SNOW FLAKES AND SCHNAPPS

SNOW FLAKES AND SCHNAPPS

JANE LAWSON

MURDOCH BOOKS

CONTENTS

INTRODUCTION 06

BABY IT'S COLD OUTSIDE 10
WARMED TO THE CORE 88
DIAMONDS AND FUR 166
DREAMING OF A WHITE CHRISTMAS 226

ACKNOWLEDGMENTS 280
INDEX 282

INTRODUCTION

I often wonder at the twist of fate that resulted in my being born and raised in Australia — I loathe the summer humidity and spend far too much time yearning for winter and the luscious, hearty, rich foods that are often only considered 'legal' at this time of year. I have been known to turn the air conditioning on to shiver mode on sweltering Christmas days, simply so I can enjoy a glass of mulled wine by the fire while awaiting a menu of crispy, crackling roast pork and stuffed turkey served with rich gravy, sweet red cabbage and potatoes roasted golden in goose fat. And let's not forget the pudding with lashings of cream and custard!

This fantasy of a white Christmas started when it was revealed to me at an early age that my paternal great-grandfather was a strong, brave Germanic sea captain. For more than two decades I was quietly proud of my German heritage and in reflective moments I would conjure images of a salty seafarer gliding through icy waters on a handsome, wooden sailing ship. In this vision, he stood on deck, steering his vessel into biting winds, his bushy, santa-like beard glistening with sea spray as he chugged potent white spirits from his hip flask. At the captain's table he laughed heartily with his crew, who would crowd around him, mesmerised by tales of his jaunts across the open seas. Dining on robust cuts of slow-cooked meat and mountains of sauerkraut, he would link arms with his crew and sway enthusiastically to bawdy sea shanties before sleeping it off in readiness for the new day. Yo ho ho!

Connecting with my German heritage seemed far more exotic than my Australian roots and I spent much of my youth gleefully anticipating the day when I would visit my homeland — a picture-perfect snow globe of castles and flower-dotted fields, black forest cake, pretzels and locals in lederhosen.

As time ticked by I attempted to dig a little deeper into my heritage. Yet despite my best efforts I kept meeting with resistance from my father's rather enormous family. Surely someone had a small snippet of information for me? Then, in my early thirties the fantasy stopped short when it was revealed to me that my beloved German seafaring great-grandfather was, in fact, a complete fabrication! As it turned out, the family myth was originated by my grandfather and perpetuated by my father, and both men took the story to their graves for reasons that shall always remain a mystery.

While my dreams were shattered, that curious white lie that was instilled in me so long ago has fuelled a fascination with frosty European countries and their respective cuisines. Of all the regions of the world I have visited, it is the snow-cloaked regions of Europe that most entrance me. Alpine villages, fairytale castles, gothic churches, rustic wooden chalets, cobbled streets, bubbling mountain streams, cowbells, twinkling Christmas markets and the sweet scents of mulled wine and roasting chestnuts have literally moved me to tears. Tiny, perfectly formed snowflake-shaped tears, naturally!

One of the resulting and delicious bi-products of my travels is the collection of recipes I return with. Over the past few years, my jaunts through Germany, Austria, Hungary, Russia, the Baltic countries of Lithuania, Latvia and Estonia, the Czech Republic, Sweden, Denmark, Finland, France, Switzerland and Italy have inspired the many recipes contained within the following pages.

Each of these countries has its own unique cuisine, and yet, as they all share borders with at least one other country (and also bearing in mind that borders have moved throughout the years), it is not surprising that their respective cuisines have merged to form unique, yet similar, dishes. For example, I had always thought that borscht was a traditional staple in Russia and the Ukraine, but as I discovered on my travels, there are similar, albeit less elaborate, beetroot soups in other parts of

Europe. Austria and Italy share the Alpine region of Tyrol, so it isn't too big a stretch to work out why you will find gnocchi-like dumplings on the Austrian side. The Hungarians make wonderful poppy seed cakes that you will also spot in Poland under a different name, perhaps containing an additional flavouring, which would never be used in a Hungarian kitchen. In Finland, people enjoy a small open pie originally from the Karelian region of Russia, while variations of mulled wine are sipped in lounge rooms from Scandinavia to Germany.

As these nations have borrowed what they undoubtedly feel are the best bits from each cuisine, making it their own, I made it my personal mission to research as many different variations for each recipe as I could in order to develop, what to my tastes, are the finest versions of each. While I am aware that purists would never appreciate such meddling, preferring to stay true to a traditional or national version of a dish, I believe these hybrid versions only help to raise the bar — after all, this is what has been happening, in a subtle way, for centuries.

In order to obtain the best results for these recipes — with as close to authentic flavours as possible — it is worth seeking out suppliers of certain European ingredients such as butter, jams and preserves, other delicatessen items and alcohol. Befriend your local butcher and fresh produce supplier and ask them to find you particular cuts or ingredients not readily available in supermarkets (although I have also given substitutions where possible). I have also been quite sympathetic to the seasonal availability of certain ingredients in colder climates, but if you have access to some of those ingredients in their fresh form, bay leaves being a good example, please do use them. On first glance you will notice that many of the recipes seem quite long, but look closer and you will find the majority are really made up of

a few smaller recipes, many of which can be made and served on their own or used to accompany other dishes. The extra time and effort to cook some of these recipes will be worth it in the end — many make large quantities, which are great for leftovers and freeze well.

The following recipes are a small but enticing selection of the vast number of dishes that I find irresistible in winter time — the pleasure being both in the preparation and the eating. The warmly spiced aromas emitted during cooking are my idea of the perfect winter atomiser. If, like me, you love winter, particularly for the season's culinary offerings, you are sure to find comfort and sustenance in the following pages.

On my fortieth birthday, just one week before this book was sent to print, I was presented with the most magnificent and unique gift — my father's youngest sister revealed to me (inadvertantly and after some personal investigation of her own) that my paternal great grandmother was in fact German! Not only that, but she hailed from a village on the very border of northern Germany and Denmark, an especially wonderful bonus as it was also a country I felt strangely at home in. I can clearly recall spotting clones of my family members around every corner and thinking that we *must* have some Nordic blood. Still overwhelmed as I write this, I can't help but feel elated by the validation and secretly pleased that my own instincts were correct — there was always something so very right about my imagined background.

In tribute to my 'memory' of my seafaring great-grandfather, my newly discovered (and, I'm honoured to say authentic) German and Danish ancestory and all my friends in frosty winter places, I hope you enjoy these recipes, which are some of the best, most craved after, sustaining, warming and comforting dishes from my mythical roots and surrounds.

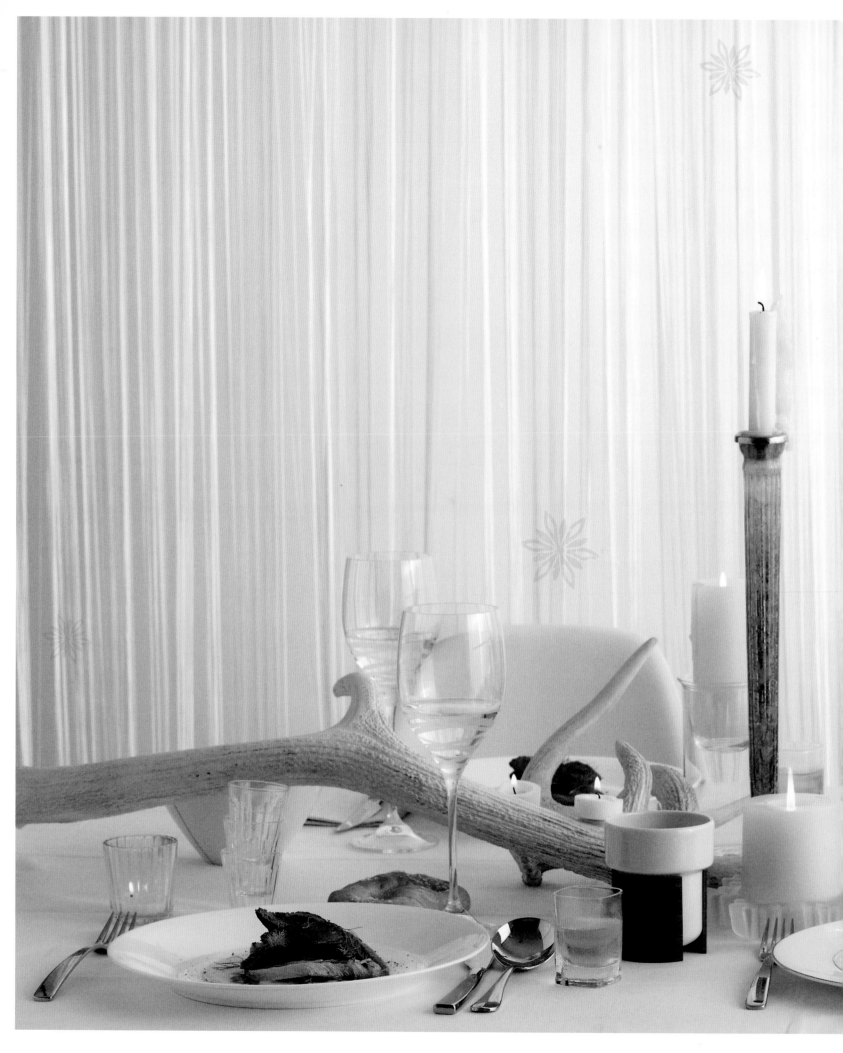

BABY IT'S COLD OUTSIDE

WHETHER YOU HAVE JUST SLIPPED FROM THE SLOPES INTO THE BAR FOR AN APRÈS SKI TREAT OR TRUDGED HOME THROUGH SLEET ON A DARK AND GRIZZLY DAY, YOU NEED SOMETHING TO TRIGGER THE THAW AND WARM YOU FROM THE INSIDE OUT. QUICKLY, WITHOUT DELAY, STEP INTO THE GLOW OF THE NEAREST COSY NOOK AND WRAP ICICLED FINGERS AROUND SOMETHING RESTORATIVELY TOASTY. SLOWLY SIP OR NIBBLE THESE SMALL BITES, SIMMERING SOUPS AND PIPING HOT LIQUID REFRESHMENTS — SOME NAUGHTY, SOME NICE!

BITTERBALLEN

SERVES 6–8

4 tablespoons butter
1 small brown onion, very finely chopped
½ celery stalk, very finely chopped
1 small carrot, very finely chopped
250 g (9 oz) minced (ground) veal
100 g (3½ oz) minced (ground) pork
2 garlic cloves, crushed
1 teaspoon finely chopped thyme
750 ml (26 fl oz/3 cups) beef stock
375 ml (13 fl oz/1½ cups) full-cream
  (whole) milk
1 bay leaf
1 teaspoon freshly squeezed lemon juice
1 large handful flat-leaf (Italian) parsley,
  finely chopped
1½ teaspoons freshly grated nutmeg
75 g (2½ oz/½ cup) plain (all-purpose) flour
320 g (11¼ oz/4 cups) fresh white breadcrumbs
3 eggs

vegetable oil, for deep-frying
a selection of mustards, for serving

Melt 1 tablespoon of the butter in a large frying pan over medium heat. Add the onion, celery and carrot and cook for 10 minutes, or until softened and lightly golden. Add the meats, garlic and thyme to the pan and cook for a further 5 minutes, breaking up any lumps with the back of a spoon, until the meat changes colour. Add the stock, milk and the bay leaf and bring to the boil, then reduce to a simmer for 1 hour 15 minutes, or until the meat is very tender. Remove from the heat, strain off the liquid and reserve. Stir the lemon juice, parsley and a few large pinches of the nutmeg into the cooked meat and set aside.

Put the remaining butter in a saucepan and melt over medium heat. Add the flour and stir for 2 minutes to combine. Gradually whisk in 310 ml (10¾ fl oz/1¼ cups) of the warm reserved cooking liquid, until smooth and completely lump-free. Allow it to come to the boil and cook for a few minutes, or until very thick. Remove from the heat and combine with the meat mixture and remaining nutmeg; season to taste. Spread the mixture out on a plate, cover with plastic wrap and refrigerate for 3 hours, or until very cold and firm.

Working quickly, roll heaped teaspoons of the mixture into neat, even-sized balls — you should make about 32 in total. Divide the breadcrumbs between two plates and lightly beat the eggs in a shallow bowl. Roll each ball in the first plate of breadcrumbs and then dip into the egg, allowing any excess to drip off. Finish by rolling each ball in the second plate of breadcrumbs. Transfer the balls to a tray and refrigerate for 2 hours, or until very cold.

Fill a deep-fryer or large heavy-based saucepan one-third with oil and heat to 180ºC (350ºF), or until a cube of bread dropped into the oil browns in 15 seconds. Deep-fry the bitterballen, in batches, for 2–3 minutes each, or until golden brown. Drain on paper towels and serve hot with mustards for dipping.

Variation: You can alter the flavour of the bitterballen slightly by adding 1½ teaspoons of curry powder. Simply stir into the lemon juice before adding to the cooked meat.

GOULASH SOUP WITH CARAWAY DUMPLINGS

SERVES 6–8

Put the bacon in a large saucepan or stockpot over medium–high heat and cook for 8 minutes, or until the bacon is slightly crisp. Remove the bacon with a slotted spoon, leaving the fat in the pan. Reduce the heat to low–medium and cook the onion for 10 minutes, or until lightly golden. Add the capsicum and carrot, along with a pinch of salt, and cook for a further 10 minutes, or until softened. Remove from the pan and set aside.

Increase the heat to medium, add the oil to the pan and cook the veal, in batches, until brown all over. Add the garlic, paprika, caraway and cayenne pepper and cook for 1 minute, stirring to coat. Add the tomato paste and wine and cook for 1 minute. Return the bacon and vegetables to the pan and stir in the stock and 500 ml (17 fl oz/ 2 cups) water. Bring to the boil, then reduce the heat and simmer for 1½–2 hours, or until the meat is tender. Skim any foam that rises to the surface.

Meanwhile, to make the dumplings, sift the flour and bicarbonate of soda together in a bowl. Stir through the caraway and ½ teaspoon salt. Whisk the egg and 1 tablespoon cold water in a separate bowl, then stir into the flour until you have a thick, soft dough, adding 1–2 teaspoons extra water if needed. Turn out onto a lightly floured surface and divide the dough in half. Roll each half into a log about 3 cm (1¼ inches) wide. Flatten slightly with the palms of your hands to square it off. Using a sharp knife, cut the log widthways into thin strips, about 3 mm (⅛ inch) thick, being careful to lift each strip of dough off the knife onto a clean, dry tea towel (dish towel). Continue this process until all of the dough is used up. Set aside for at least 30 minutes.

When the soup is almost ready, drop the dumplings into the simmering soup and cook for 5 minutes, or until they rise to the surface. Cook for a further 2 minutes. Stir in the parsley, season to taste and serve immediately.

Variation: If you prefer, omit the dumplings and increase the caraway in the soup to 1 teaspoon and add 2 diced floury potatoes towards the end of cooking instead. You can also add a dollop of sour cream to serve if you wish.

3 streaky bacon slices, diced
2 brown onions, chopped
2 red capsicums (peppers), diced
1 large carrot, finely diced
2 tablespoons olive oil
1 kg (2 lb 4 oz) veal stewing meat (such as round steak), cut into 1.5 cm (⅝ in) dice
2 garlic cloves, crushed
2 tablespoons Hungarian sweet paprika
½ teaspoon caraway seeds, toasted and ground
a pinch of cayenne pepper
1½ tablespoons tomato paste (concentrated purée)
250 ml (9 fl oz/1 cup) red wine
2 litres (70 fl oz/8 cups) beef stock
1 handful flat-leaf (Italian) parsley, finely chopped

CARAWAY DUMPLINGS

150 g (5½ oz/1 cup) plain (all-purpose) flour
¼ teaspoon bicarbonate of soda (baking soda)
1 teaspoon caraway seeds, toasted and lightly crushed
1 egg

CHEESE FONDUE

SERVES 6

1 garlic clove, bruised
250 ml (9 fl oz/1 cup) dry, sparkling
  white wine, preferably Swiss Neuchâtel
  or Champagne
300 g (10½ oz) gruyère cheese, finely diced
200 g (7 oz) emmental cheese, finely diced
3 teaspoons cornflour (cornstarch)
1½ tablespoons Kirsch, or other
  mild-flavoured white spirit
freshly grated nutmeg, to taste

FOR DIPPING
cubes of firm bread, such as baguette, rye or
  pumpernickel
meat, such as cubes of ham and pieces
  of salami or small cooked prawns (shrimp),
  for dipping
vegetables, such as slices of raw crisp fennel,
  capsicum or carrot, or lightly cooked baby
  potatoes, mushrooms or asparagus tips
pickles, such as cornichons, caperberries or
  pickled onions

Rub all around the inside of a fondue pot with the bruised garlic clove, then discard. Add 185 ml (6 fl oz/¾ cup) of the wine to the fondue pot and place the pot over a lit fondue base (this should be in the middle of the table you are eating at). (See the manufacturer's instructions on how to set up the fondue set.) Bring the wine to a slow simmer over the flame.

Toss the cheeses in a bowl with the cornflour and add a small handful of cheese to the pot. Stir in a figure eight pattern until the cheese starts to melt, then add another handful of cheese and continue with this method, always stirring in a figure eight, until all the cheese is melted and smooth. Be patient with this step, as the mixture will firm up first before it melts into a smooth sauce. Continue stirring while gradually adding the Kirsch. Season with the grated nutmeg and freshly ground black pepper, to taste.

The fondue should be kept just lightly bubbling at all times so the cheese doesn't overheat and become stringy. You may need to turn the heat off for a short time to achieve this, but remember to return to a low heat once it starts to cool down. The cheese mixture will thicken as the quantity is reduced — you can thin it out by adding a little of the remaining wine, but warm it slightly first.

Using fondue forks, or other long-handled forks, spear the bread, meat or vegetables one at a time, and dip them into the cheese, swirling to coat — the continuous stirring helps to keep the right consistency.

Nibble on the pickles between bites to help cut through the richness of the cheese. Do not be tempted to drink cold drinks, including wine, throughout or just after the meal, as it will cause the cheese to set firmly in your stomach, making it more difficult to digest. Instead, drink small glasses of Kirsch or whichever spirit you are using in the fondue.

Variations: Try additional flavours, such as: mustard, paprika or cayenne pepper; truffles, finely chopped and sautéed in a little butter can be added to the fondue when it is ready to eat.

Notes: Use a wine with noticeable acid, as this helps to melt the cheese — if it still needs assistance, add ½ teaspoon lemon juice.

ROSEMARY AND SPICE CHESTNUTS, ALMONDS AND HAZELNUTS

SERVES 6

Preheat the oven to 180°C (350°F/Gas 4). Using a small, sharp knife, cut a small slit in the rounded stem end of each chestnut. Put the chestnuts in a saucepan with the stock and 250 ml (9 fl oz/1 cup) water and bring to the boil. Cook for 15 minutes, then drain. When cool enough to handle, peel the chestnuts starting at the cut end.

Put the butter, honey, allspice, rosemary and fennel in a large ovenproof frying pan and place over medium heat until the butter has melted. Remove from the heat, add the chestnuts, hazelnuts and almonds, and toss to coat. Place the pan in the oven and cook for 20–25 minutes, stirring occasionally, until the chestnuts are tender and the other nuts are golden. Remove from the oven, sprinkle with sea salt and toss to combine.

Allow the nuts to cool until they are just warm and a little crisp, before serving in the pan as nibbles to have with drinks.

500 g (1 lb 2 oz) fresh chestnuts
500 ml (17 fl oz/2 cups) chicken or beef stock
2 tablespoons butter
2 tablespoons honey
⅛ teaspoon ground allspice
1 rosemary sprig, finely chopped
½ teaspoon ground fennel
35 g (1¼ oz/¼ cup) whole hazelnuts
40 g (1½ oz/¼ cup) whole blanched almonds
1 teaspoon sea salt

BORSCHT WITH HORSERADISH CREAM

SERVES 6–8

3 x 200 g (7 oz) beetroot (beets)

1 tablespoon olive oil

1 kg (2 lb 4 oz) beef short ribs

1 large brown onion, chopped

1 large carrot, finely chopped

2 teaspoons caraway seeds

4 garlic cloves, finely chopped

1 teaspoon ground allspice, plus ¼ teaspoon
  extra

1 bay leaf

1 teaspoon dried porcini (cep) mushrooms,
  crumbled

3 litres (105 fl oz/12 cups) beef stock

400 g (14 oz/1⅔ cups) tinned chopped tomatoes

½ small red cabbage, shredded

1 tablespoon cider vinegar or red wine vinegar

1 teaspoon soft brown sugar

1 large handful dill, chopped

HORSERADISH CREAM

125 g (4½ oz/½ cup) sour cream

1 tablespoon freshly grated horseradish
  or horseradish relish

Rinse the beetroot well, scrubbing off any dirt. Place in a large saucepan and cover generously with water. Bring to the boil and cook for 2 hours, or until the beetroot are tender when deeply pierced with a small, sharp knife. Remove from the heat and allow to cool completely in the cooking liquid.

Meanwhile, heat the olive oil in a large saucepan or stockpot over medium–high heat. Cook the beef short ribs, in batches, until brown, then remove the ribs to a plate. Add the onion, carrot and caraway seeds to the pan and sauté until the onion is lightly golden. Add the garlic, 1 teaspoon allspice and the bay leaf and cook for 30 seconds. Return the beef to the pan and mix in the mushrooms, stock, tomatoes, cabbage and vinegar. Bring to the boil, then reduce the heat and simmer for 2 hours, or until the meat is very tender. Turn off the heat. Remove the ribs and set aside to cool slightly before pulling the beef from the bones. Discard the bones. Chop the meat into small, bite-sized pieces and return to the pot.

Drain the cooled beetroot, reserving the cooking liquid. Wearing rubber gloves, peel the beetroot and then roughly grate them into a bowl. Pour the reserved cooking liquid through a very fine sieve into the soup pot and add the grated beetroot. Stir well to combine, then place over high heat and bring to the boil. Stir in the sugar and extra allspice, then sprinkle over the dill; season to taste.

To make the horseradish cream, combine the sour cream and the horseradish in a bowl. Serve the borscht hot, with a dollop of horseradish cream on top. Don't forget a shot of Russian vodka on the side!

HERBED PRETZELS WITH HONEY-GLAZED HAM AND MUSTARD BUTTER

MAKES 12

PRETZELS

1 tablespoon active dried yeast

1 tablespoon soft brown sugar

600 g (1 lb 5 oz/4 cups) strong flour or plain (all-purpose) flour

2 tablespoons melted butter

310 ml (10¾ fl oz/1¼ cups) warm full-cream (whole) milk

1 large handful dill, finely chopped

½ teaspoon dried marjoram or thyme

2 tablespoons bicarbonate of soda (baking soda)

coarsely ground sea salt

Combine the yeast, sugar and 3 tablespoons warm water in a small dish. Cover with plastic wrap and set aside for 15 minutes, or until frothy.

Sift the flour and 1 teaspoon salt into a bowl, make a well in the centre, and pour in the yeast mixture along with the butter, milk, dill and marjoram or thyme. Mix with a wooden spoon to form a moderately stiff dough. Turn out onto a lightly floured surface and knead for 5 minutes, or until smooth. Place in a large, oiled bowl. Cover with a tea towel (dish towel) and place in a large plastic bag. Don't seal the bag tightly or fold it over; the dough needs room to expand. Place in a warm, draught-free place (near a warm oven, for example) for 50–60 minutes, or until doubled in size. Punch down, then cover and rest again for about 15 minutes.

Preheat the oven to 200°C (400°F/Gas 6). Grease two baking trays. Transfer the dough to a lightly floured work surface and divide into 12 even portions. Roll each portion between your hand and the work surface to form a rope, about 1.5 cm (⅝ inch) thick. To form the pretzels, place a dough rope horizontally in front of you. Take both ends and gently pull towards you so that the rope forms a curve. Cross one end over the other, like you are about to form a loose knot, but moving back away from your body, tuck both ends under the curved side to form a pretzel shape. Place onto the prepared trays and continue to fold pretzels with the remaining dough ropes.

Combine the bicarbonate of soda with 1 litre (35 fl oz/4 cups) hot water in a deep dish, stirring until completely dissolved. Dip each pretzel into the solution, then briefly rest on paper towels to soak up any excess liquid. Return the pretzels to the trays, spacing them a little apart. Sprinkle with the sea salt and allow to rest and rise for a further 10 minutes. Bake in the oven for 25–30 minutes, or until deep golden all over.

Meanwhile, to make the mustard butter, combine the butter and the two mustards well and then spoon into a small serving dish.

To cook the ham, heat the butter in a large frying pan over medium-high heat until it sizzles. Add the ham slices, a few at a time, cooking until lightly golden, then remove from the pan. Add the honey, cider vinegar and 2 tablespoons water and bring to the boil. Cook for 1 minute, or until thick and glazy, then return the ham to the pan and toss to coat the ham well.

Take the pan to the table with the hot pretzels and the mustard butter. Give each person a small serrated knife to cut through their pretzels so they can make sandwiches with the mustard butter and ham.

Tip: If short on time, just buy large soft pretzels and warm them up before serving.

MUSTARD BUTTER
125 g (4½ oz/½ cup) butter, softened
1 tablespoon wholegrain mustard
2 teaspoons hot mustard

HONEY-GLAZED HAM
1 tablespoon butter
750 g (1 lb 10 oz) small, thick ham slices from the bone
90 g (3¼ oz/¼ cup) honey
1 tablespoon cider vinegar

POTATO FLATBREADS WITH SMOKED SALMON

MAKES 8

PICKLED CUCUMBERS

1 teaspoon caster (superfine) sugar
1½ tablespoons white wine vinegar
1 handful fresh dill, finely chopped
2 small firm short cucumbers, very
   finely sliced

EGG AND ANCHOVY BUTTER

2 hard-boiled eggs, finely chopped
3 tablespoons butter, softened
1 anchovy, very finely chopped
2 teaspoons capers in vinegar, drained
   and finely chopped
½ handful fresh chives, snipped

FLATBREADS

2 large (about 400 g/14 oz) all-purpose
   potatoes, such as desiree
2 tablespoons butter, melted, plus extra,
   for greasing
2½ tablespoons pouring (whipping) cream
½ teaspoon caster (superfine) sugar
120g (4¼ oz/¾ cup) plain (all-purpose) flour
16 slices smoked salmon, to serve

To make the pickled cucumbers, combine the sugar, vinegar, dill and ½ teaspoon salt in a non-metallic bowl and stir until the sugar has dissolved. Add the cucumber slices and toss well. Cover with plastic wrap and refrigerate until the flatbreads are ready to serve.

To make the egg and anchovy butter, place the eggs, butter and anchovy in a bowl and mash together until smooth. Stir through the capers and chives and season with freshly ground black pepper. Set aside in a serving dish. If making in advance, refrigerate until ready to serve, but bring to room temperature before serving.

To make the flatbreads, put the washed but not peeled potatoes in a saucepan of water and bring to the boil. Cook for 20 minutes, or until tender, then drain. When cool enough to handle, peel and mash well, then mix through the melted butter and cream. Quickly mix in the sugar, 1 teaspoon salt and enough flour to make a soft, slightly sticky dough.

Divide the dough into eight even portions and put them on a tray, lightly covering them with plastic wrap to prevent them from drying out as you work. On a lightly floured work surface, roll out one dough ball into a round until it is as thin as possible without tearing, about 3 mm (⅛ inch) thick.

Heat a large non-stick frying pan over medium heat. Lightly brush with melted butter. Carefully transfer the flatbread to the pan and cook for 2 minutes or until large bubbles appear on the surface and darkish spots start to appear on the underside.

Carefully turn it over and cook for 1 minute further, then transfer to a warmed serving dish and cover with clean tea towels (dish towels) to keep warm. Continue with the remaining dough, rolling a new round while each flatbread is cooking. (If you feel confident, heat two frying pans so you can cook two flatbreads at a time.)

Once all the flatbreads are cooked, serve them immediately at the table with the egg and anchovy butter, smoked salmon and pickled cucumbers, so that diners can make their own wraps.

MUSSELS IN A FENNEL-SCENTED BROTH

SERVES 4–6

Scrub and debeard the mussels, discarding any that are cracked. Tap any open mussels on a bench; if they don't close, throw them away as they are dead. Refrigerate the mussels until ready to use.

Melt the butter in a large saucepan or stockpot over medium heat. Add the bacon, leek, fennel, carrot and celeriac and cook, stirring occasionally, for 10 minutes, or until softened. Add the garlic and spices and cook for a further 1 minute. Increase the heat to high, add the stock and Akvavit and bring to the boil. Cook for 5 minutes.

Add the mussels to the pan, cover, and cook over high heat for about 5–6 minutes, shaking the pan occasionally. Discard any mussels that do not open. Add half of the reserved fennel fronds and season, to taste. Spoon the mussels and broth into deep bowls and garnish with the remaining fennel fronds. Serve with a dollop of crème fraîche and some crusty or rye bread, if desired, for mopping up the juices. And don't forget the shots of Akvavit!

Variation: For a creamy soup base, remove the mussels from the pan once cooked, discarding any that do not open. Stir the crème fraîche through the broth before returning the opened mussels to the pan.

Note: Akvavit (Aquavit) is an alcoholic beverage originating in Scandinavia. It is distilled from either potato or grain and is usually flavoured with a combination of spices, including caraway seeds, anise, dill, fennel and coriander.

2 kg (4 lb 8 oz) mussels

1 tablespoon butter

2 streaky bacon slices, finely chopped

1 leek, white part only, finely sliced

½ fennel bulb (about150 g/5 ½ oz), finely diced, plus feathery fennel fronds chopped and reserved for garnish

1 carrot, finely diced

200 g (7 oz) celeriac, finely diced

2 garlic cloves, crushed

½ teaspoon ground fennel

½ teaspoon caraway seeds

½ teaspoon ground cumin

1 litre (35 fl oz/4 cups) home-made or good-quality fish stock from your local fishmonger

60 ml (2 fl oz/¼ cup) Akvavit (Aquavit) (see note) or aniseed-flavoured spirit

125 g (4½ oz/½ cup) crème fraîche

KARELIAN OPEN PIES

MAKES 12

RICE FILLING
140 g (5 oz/⅔ cup) short-grain rice
375 ml (13 fl oz/1½ cups) full-cream (whole)
  milk
3 tablespoons butter
2 egg yolks
50 g (1¾ oz) ham or cooked or smoked salmon,
  thinly sliced
100 g (3½ oz) lappi or edam cheese, grated
1 spring onion (scallion), finely chopped

RYE CRUST
300 g (10½ oz/3 cups) rye flour (see note)
1 teaspoon caraway seeds, toasted
⅛ teaspoon ground coriander
1½ tablespoons vegetable oil
1 tablespoon butter, melted

egg and anchovy butter (page 26), to serve
  (optional)

Put the rice and 310 ml (10¾ oz/1¼ cups) water in a large saucepan over high heat and bring to the boil. Reduce the heat and simmer, uncovered, for 20 minutes, or until most of the water has been absorbed. Stir in the milk, cover, and simmer for a further 20 minutes, or until the milk has been absorbed to form a thick rice porridge. Remove from the heat, stir in the butter and set aside to cool completely. Add the egg yolks, ham or salmon, cheese and spring onion to the rice mixture and combine well. Season to taste.

To make the pastry, sift the flour into a bowl and stir through the spices and ½ teaspoon salt. Alternating small amounts of both, mix in 150 ml (5 fl oz) water and the combined oil and butter, to form a compact dough. Divide the dough into 12 even-sized pieces, then use your hands to shape into balls. On a lightly floured work surface, roll out the balls as thinly as possible into circles with a 12 cm (4½ inch) diameter. Cover the with plastic wrap as you work, to prevent them from drying out.

Place 1½ rounded tablespoons of rice filling in the centre of each circle and spread out, leaving a 2 cm (¾ inch) border. Fold the pastry border upwards, and pinch around the top rim to scallop the edge around the filling. Pinch together at two opposite sides to form an oval shape. Arrange the pastries on baking trays lined with baking paper, spacing them 2 cm (¾ inch) apart and refrigerate for at least 20 minutes, or until ready to cook.

Preheat the oven to 220°C (425°F/Gas 7). Bake the pies for 10 minutes, or until the pastry is firm and the filling is lightly golden. Serve hot with a pot of the egg and anchovy butter alongside, if desired, for dolloping over.

Variation: These pies can also be filled with a mashed potato or carrot mixture instead of rice.

Note: Only use light-coloured and fine-textured rye flour; if this is not available, use a mixture of half rye flour and half plain (all-purpose) flour.

STICKY PLUM AND FENNEL PORK RIBS

SERVES 6

2.5 kg (5 lb 8 oz) pork sparerib racks
125 ml (4 fl oz/½ cup) Slivovica (Polish plum
   brandy), plus 1 tablespoon extra
60 ml (2 fl oz/¼ cup) cider vinegar
2 teaspoons ground fennel seeds
½ teaspoon ground ginger
¾ teaspoon ground caraway
½ teaspoon ground allspice
¼ teaspoon dried marjoram
¼ teaspoon white pepper
5 garlic cloves, bruised
2 large brown onions, sliced
3 bacon slices, roughly chopped
2 tablespoons honey
105 g (3½ oz/⅓ cup) plum conserve or
   good-quality jam

Cut the pork racks into three-rib-wide pieces. Combine the Slivovica, vinegar, spices, marjoram and garlic in a large non-metallic bowl, then add the ribs and toss well to coat. Cover tightly with plastic wrap and refrigerate for at least 6 hours, or overnight, tossing occasionally to evenly distribute the marinade.

Preheat the oven to 180°C (350°F/Gas 4). Scatter the onion and bacon over the base of a large roasting tin. Place the ribs, meaty side down, in a single layer over the onions. Drizzle any marinade over the top and add 1.5 litres (52 fl oz/6 cups) water, or enough to cover the ribs. Cover tightly with foil and bake in the oven for 2 hours, or until the meat is tender. Remove from the oven and increase the temperature to 220°C (425°F/Gas 7).

Transfer the ribs to a plate and set aside. Remove the onion and bacon mixture and discard (or alternatively, reserve it for adding to a cabbage or potato side dish to serve with the ribs).

Line the cleaned tin with a large piece of foil for catching any drips and place a large wire rack over the top. Place the ribs, meaty side up, on the rack in a single layer.

Combine the extra Slivovica, honey and plum conserve in a bowl and stir in 1 tablespoon warm water, whisking until smooth. Brush to cover the ribs and cook in the oven for 30 minutes, basting regularly with the plum mixture until dark and sticky. Transfer to a platter and serve drizzled with the basting liquid.

Tip: Serve with small bowls filled with warm water and a splash of cider vinegar for cleaning sticky fingers.

DILLED CHICKEN AND VEGETABLE BROTH WITH NOODLES

SERVES 8

Preheat the oven to 190ºC (375ºF/Gas 5). Put the chicken bones and onion in a baking dish, drizzle with a little olive oil and sprinkle with salt. Cook for 40 minutes, or until a deep golden colour. Tip into a large saucepan or stockpot and add 6 litres (210 fl oz) water, the garlic and bay leaves. Bring to the boil, reduce to a rapid simmer and cook for 1½ hours, skimming any foam that comes to the top. Remove from the heat, strain the liquid and return it to the pan. Discard the solids.

Rinse the chicken inside and out and place in the pan with the leek, kohlrabi, swede, carrot, celery and celeriac. Bring to the boil over high heat, then reduce to a simmer and cook for 40 minutes. Carefully remove the chicken from the pan and set aside until just cool enough to handle. Allow the stock to gently simmer.

Bring a large saucepan of salted water to the boil, add the noodles and cook according to the packet instructions, until *al dente*. Drain and add to the simmering stock along with the peas. Stir, then allow to cook until the peas are tender. Meanwhile, remove and discard the chicken skin. Shred the meat. Return the meat to the pot and add the dill, chives and parsley. Season to taste and serve immediately.

1 kg (2 lb 4 oz) chicken bones (available at poultry suppliers and good butchers)
1 brown onion, chopped
olive oil, for drizzling
3 garlic cloves, bruised
2 fresh bay leaves
1.5 kg (3 lb 5 oz) whole chicken
1 leek, white part only, finely sliced
1 small kohlrabi, diced
2 small swedes (rutabaga) or parsnip (about 300 g/10½ oz), diced
2 carrots, diced
2 celery stalks, diced
1 small celeriac, diced
200 g (7 oz) thin, dried egg noodles or spaghettini
80 g (2¾ oz/½ cup) fresh or frozen peas
3 tablespoons finely chopped dill
½ handful chives, snipped
½ bunch flat-leaf (Italian) parsley, chopped

SPICY SPLIT PEA SOUP WITH SMOKED HAM

SERVES 4–6

500 g (1 lb 2 oz/2¼ cups) yellow or green split
  peas
3 tablespoons butter
1 large brown onion, chopped
1 large carrot, diced
1 celery stalk, diced
1 smoked ham hock (about
  750 g/1 lb 10 oz)
1 handful of celery leaves, finely chopped
1 thyme sprig, leaves finely chopped
1 marjoram sprig, finely chopped
a pinch of ground cloves
60 ml (2 fl oz/¼ cup) cider vinegar, plus
  1 tablespoon extra
3 teaspoons hot mustard

Soak the split peas in plenty of cold water overnight. Drain and set aside.

Melt half the butter in a large saucepan or stockpot over medium heat and cook the onion, carrot and celery for 5 minutes, or until softened. Add the split peas, ham hock, celery leaves, thyme, marjoram, celery stalk, vinegar and 2.5 litres (88 fl oz/10 cups) water. Bring to the boil over high heat, then reduce the heat and simmer for 3 hours, or until the ham is starting to fall off the hock. Skim off any scum that rises to the surface during cooking. Remove the hock and when cool enough to handle, discard the skin and bone, shred the meat and set aside.

Add the mustard and remaining butter to the soup and purée, in batches, with a stick blender or in a food processor, until smooth. Return to the pan and gently reheat. Return the shredded ham to the pan and stir to combine. Season to taste and stir through the extra vinegar.

Serve hot with crisp or rye bread and butter. Soup will thicken on standing. Add extra stock and vinegar upon reheating, if needed.

Variation: You can add sausages like kielbasa, or fresh or pickled pork meat to the soup instead of the ham hock.

RICH ONION SOUP WITH CHEESE TOASTS

SERVES 6

Melt the butter in a large saucepan over medium heat. Add the onions and stir to coat in the butter. Cook, stirring regularly, for 5 minutes, or until softened. Reduce the heat to low and cook for 30–40 minutes more, stirring occasionally, until dark golden in colour.

Add the thyme, bay leaf and stock, increase the heat to high and bring to the boil. Reduce to a simmer and cook for 45 minutes. Stir through the Cognac and cream, if using, and cook for a few minutes longer to cook off the alcohol. Stir in the nutmeg and season to taste.

Just before the soup has finished cooking, prepare the toasts. Preheat a grill (broiler) to high and toast the bread on both sides until lightly golden. Rub one side of the toast with the cut garlic then place, garlic side up, in a single layer on a baking tray lined with baking paper. Combine the cheeses and evenly divide among the toasts. Place under the grill and cook until the cheese is bubbling and golden. Sprinkle the thyme leaves over the toasts. Ladle the soup into six wide shallow soup bowls and float one toast, cheese side up, on top of each.

Variation: A slightly different version, with a more subtle flavour, can be achieved by only softening the onions, not allowing them to brown, and substituting half of the stock with milk.

100 g (3½ oz) butter

5 large brown onions (about 1 kg/2 lb 4 oz), sliced

1 thyme sprig

1 bay leaf

1.5 litres (52 fl oz/6 cups) home-made or good-quality veal or beef stock

2 teaspoons Cognac, or brandy

60 ml (2 fl oz/¼ cup) pouring (whipping) cream (optional)

¼ teaspoon freshly grated nutmeg

6 thick slices of day-old baguette or sourdough bread

2 garlic cloves, cut in half

100 g (3½ oz/¾ cup) grated gruyère cheese

25 g (1 oz/¼ cup) grated parmesan cheese

thyme leaves, to garnish

SWEDISH OPEN BURGER WITH BEETROOT SALAD

SERVES 4

FISH CAKES

250 g (9 oz) skinless, boneless, firm white
  fish fillets, such as perch
250 g (9 oz) minced (ground) veal
1 small brown onion, grated and squeezed
  to extract excess moisture
1 garlic clove, crushed
165 g (5¾ oz/2 cups) fresh white breadcrumbs
90 g (3¼ oz/⅓ cup) sour cream
1 handful flat-leaf (Italian) parsley,
  finely chopped
1 thyme sprig, leaves finely chopped
¼ teaspoon freshly grated nutmeg
a large pinch of ground caraway
a large pinch of white pepper
1 teaspoon finely grated lemon zest

BEETROOT SALAD

1 cooked beetroot (beet) (about 200g/7 oz)
1 tablespoon Akvavit (Aquavit)
  (see note, page 29)
1 small handful dill, finely chopped
2 teaspoons capers in vinegar, drained
  and chopped
a large pinch of ground allspice
1 teaspoon grated horseradish
2 teaspoons cider vinegar, or to taste
1 tablespoon butter
2 tablespoons vegetable oil
4 thick slices white or light rye bread
4 slices Hushallsost or Port-Salut cheese

Roughly chop the fish fillets and then mince in a food processor using the pulse button until the finely chopped bits just come together. Transfer the fish to a bowl and combine well with the veal, onion, garlic, breadcrumbs, sour cream, herbs, spices and lemon zest. Cover with plastic wrap and refrigerate for 4–6 hours.

Meanwhile, to make the beetroot salad, roughly grate the beetroot and combine with the Akvavit, dill, capers, allspice, horseradish and vinegar. Season to taste and set aside.

When ready to cook, remove the fish mixture from the fridge and season with salt, mixing well. Shape into four oval fish cakes, about 1.5 cm (⅝ inch) thick — they will be about 8 cm (3¼ inches) long and 6 cm (2½ inches) wide. Heat the butter and oil in a large frying pan over medium heat. Add the patties to the pan and cook for 5 minutes on each side, or until they are just cooked through and golden on the outside.

Meanwhile, preheat a grill (broiler) to high and lightly toast the bread on both sides. Top each slice with a slice of cheese and place a cooked fish cake on top. Add a dollop of the beetroot salad and serve immediately.

TARTIFLETTE

SERVES 4

Preheat the oven to 240°C (475°F/Gas 8). Cut the jambon into 1 x 3 cm (½ x 1¼ inch) strips and place in a large cast-iron frying pan over medium heat. Cook for 10 minutes or until the fat has melted away from the meat. Remove the jambon with a slotted spoon and drain on paper towel, leaving the rendered fat in the pan.

Add the potato and onion to the pan, increase the heat to medium–high and cook for 5 minutes, or until the onion has softened. Add the thyme and mushrooms and cook for 5 minutes, or until the mushrooms are starting to wilt. Add the wine and increase the heat to high. Bring to the boil and cook for 1 minute. Remove from the heat, stir in the crème fraîche, reserved jambon and garlic; season to taste.

Dice the cheese and sprinkle over the top. Place in the oven and cook for 10 minutes, then reduce the temperature to 190°C (375°F/ Gas 5) and cook for a further 30 minutes, or until the potato is tender when pierced with the tip of a knife.

Serve on its own or with a crisp green salad.

Note: Reblochon is a creamy French cheese traditionally used in the luscious French tartiflette, but if not available, suitable substitutes include firm brie, Vacherin, raclette, taleggio or fontina.

200 g (7 oz) jambon or prosciutto, in one piece

1 kg (2 lb 4 oz) all-purpose potatoes, such as desiree, peeled and cut into 1½ cm (¾ inch) slices, then halved crossways

1 brown onion, chopped

1 teaspoon thyme, finely chopped

150 g (5½ oz) sliced seasonal mushrooms, such as porcini (cep)

125 ml (4 fl oz/½ cup) dry white wine

250 g (9 oz/1 cup) crème fraîche

1 garlic clove, finely chopped

500 g (1 lb 2 oz) Reblochon, rind removed (see note)

BEER-COOKED BRATWURST HOT DOGS WITH SWEET AND SPICY MUSTARD

SERVES 6

MUSTARD (Make mustard 1 week in advance)
6 tablespoons yellow mustard seeds
60 ml (2 fl oz/¼ cup) cider vinegar
1 bay leaf
1 tablespoon grated brown onion
2 garlic cloves, crushed
½ teaspoon ground allspice
¾ teaspoon ground cinnamon
a small pinch of cayenne pepper
2 tablespoons soft brown sugar

6 good-quality bratwurst sausages
   (about 100 g/3½ oz each)
1 tablespoon butter
2 brown onions, thinly sliced
250 ml (9 fl oz/1 cup) German wheat beer
6 long home-made or good-quality bread rolls
softened butter, for spreading
mayonnaise, to serve (optional)
tomato sauce (ketchup), to serve (optional)

To make the mustard, soak the mustard seeds in cold water overnight. Rinse and drain well, then lightly grind using a mortar and pestle to break up the seeds. Put in a saucepan with the vinegar, bay leaf, onion, garlic, spices and 375 ml (13 fl oz/1½ cups) water and bring to the boil. Reduce the heat and simmer for 25 minutes, stirring constantly, until the mustard is thick. Add the sugar and 1½ teaspoons salt and stir until the sugar has dissolved. Transfer to a clean glass jar while the mustard is still hot and seal with a tight-fitting lid. When cool, store in the refrigerator for at least 1 week before using. The mustard will keep for up to 2 months.

To cook the bratwurst sausages, brush a heavy-based frying pan with a little oil and heat over medium heat. Prick each sausage once and add to the pan. Turn in the pan so that the outside just changes colour. Add the butter and onions and cook for 10 minutes, or until the onions are lightly golden. Add the beer and 125 ml (4 fl oz/½ cup) water and cook, stirring the onions and turning the sausages occasionally, for about 10 minutes, or until the sausages are cooked through and tender.

Butter the rolls, and fill each with a sausage and onions. Serve the mustard, mayonnaise and tomato sauce, if using, on the side.

Variation: Use different sausages, such as white, spicy, Polish kielbasa, or Scandinavian sausages. You can also use a good-quality store-bought mustard if you are short on time.

MUSHROOM AND BARLEY SOUP WITH PICKLED MUSHROOM CREAM

SERVES 4–6

Thoroughly rinse the barley, then soak in water overnight. Drain well.

Heat the butter and oil in a large saucepan or stockpot over medium heat. Add the onion, carrot and celery and cook, stirring occasionally, until lightly golden. Add the field mushrooms and garlic, stir to combine, and cook for 5 minutes, or until the mushrooms have wilted. Add the crumbled dried mushroom, bay leaf, thyme, allspice, white pepper and herring and stir to combine. Add the stock and bring to the boil over high heat. Cook for 30 minutes, then add the barley and potato. Bring to the boil again, then reduce the heat and simmer for 30 minutes, or until the barley is tender. Season to taste.

Meanwhile, to make the pickled mushroom cream, combine the chopped mushrooms, vinegar, garlic, white pepper and a couple of large pinches of salt. Set aside for 1 hour to allow the flavours to develop. Combine the mushroom mixture with the sour cream and herbs and refrigerate until ready to use. Serve the hot soup with a dollop of mushroom cream.

210 g (7½ oz) pearl barley

2 tablespoons butter

1 tablespoon vegetable oil

1 large brown onion, chopped

1 large carrot, finely diced

2 celery stalks, finely diced

400 g (14 oz) field mushrooms, finely chopped

2 garlic cloves, crushed

a few slices of dried porcini (cep) mushroom, crumbled

1 bay leaf

1 thyme sprig, leaves finely chopped

¼ teaspoon ground allspice

¼ teaspoon white pepper

1 whole pickled herring (about 100 g/3½ oz), soaked in cold water for 1 hour, or 2 anchovies, very finely chopped

2 litres (70 fl oz/8 cups) veal or chicken stock

1 large floury potato, finely diced

PICKLED MUSHROOM CREAM

100 g (3½ oz) button mushrooms, finely chopped

2 tablespoons white wine vinegar

2 garlic cloves, crushed

⅛ teaspoon white pepper

125 g (4½ oz/½ cup) sour cream

a small handful of dill, chopped

a handful of flat-leaf (Italian) parsley, chopped

PAN-FRIED SANDWICHES

SERVES 4

8 thin slices of day-old crusty Italian bread (from the middle of the loaf)
softened butter, for spreading
2 tablespoons mustard fruits, very finely chopped
1 small spring onion (scallion), finely chopped
120 g (4¼ oz) sliced provolone, fontina or mozzarella cheese
120 g (4¼ oz) thinly sliced salami or prosciutto
3 large eggs
60 ml (2 fl oz/¼ cup) full-cream (whole) milk
1 oregano sprig, leaves finely chopped
a pinch of freshly grated nutmeg
1 tablespoon butter, plus extra for frying
2 tablespoons olive oil

Butter all the bread slices on one side only and place on a work surface, buttered side up. Combine the mustard fruits and spring onion and sprinkle over four of the slices of buttered bread. Top with half of the cheese slices, then the salami or prosciutto, and then the remaining cheese. Take the other four slices of bread and place on top of the cheese, butter side down, pressing down firmly to make four sandwiches.

Whisk together the eggs, milk, oregano and nutmeg until well combined. Season with salt and freshly ground black pepper, then pour into a deep, wide bowl or a small baking dish.

Heat half of the butter and olive oil in a large frying pan over medium heat. Holding each sandwich together, carefully dip each side into the egg mixture, allowing any excess to drip off. Place two sandwiches in the frying pan at a time, and cook for 4 minutes on each side, or until golden. Remove from the pan and rest on paper towel to absorb excess moisture. Keep warm in a low oven. Wipe out the pan and heat the remaining butter and oil and cook the remaining sandwiches. Serve immediately.

Variations: Pan-fried sandwiches are popular in many European countries. You could omit the oregano from the egg mix and try one of the following, or your own choice of fillings:

- Havarti or ridder cheese, cured ham and honey mustard.
- Thick cream cheese with gravlax or smoked salmon and capers or dill pickles. For this option, use a soft rye bread and add a little dill to the eggs.
- Norwegian goat's cheese (gjoest) with lingonberry preserves and air-dried venison slices.
- Mozzarella with garlicky pan-fried mushroom slices and olives.
- French jambon with gruyère cheese and Dijon mustard.

WINTER VEGETABLE CRUMBLE

SERVES 6

Preheat the oven to 190°C (375°F/Gas 5). Lightly grease six 1½-cup gratin dishes or ramekins. Cut the carrots, celeriac, parsnip and sweet potato into 1.5 cm (⅝ inch) dice. Half-fill a saucepan with water and bring to the boil. Add the vegetables and cook for about 5 minutes, or until just tender. Drain, reserving the cooking liquid. Set the vegetables aside.

Melt half of the butter in a saucepan over medium–high heat. Add the bay leaf and pancetta and cook for a few minutes, or until the pancetta is starting to brown lightly. Add the spring onion whites and cook for 3 minutes, or until softened, then remove the mixture from the pan and set aside with the vegetables.

Melt the remaining butter in the pan and add the flour, stirring well to combine. Gradually add 185 ml (6 fl oz/¾ cup) of the reserved vegetable cooking liquid, stirring until smooth. Carefully stir in the crème fraîche until smooth, then add the garlic and nutmeg and season with salt and a little freshly ground black pepper. Add the vegetable mixture and the spring onion greens and mix well. Divide the mixture between the prepared dishes.

To make the topping, rub the butter into the flour with your fingertips until the mixture resembles breadcrumbs. Stir in the ground almonds, parmesan and rosemary. Divide the topping evenly over the vegetables and cook in the oven for 25 minutes, or until the crumble is golden. Serve with a green salad.

2 carrots
½ small celeriac
1 parsnip
1 small white or orange sweet potato
1 tablespoon butter
1 bay leaf
100 g (3½ oz) pancetta, finely diced
4 spring onions (scallions), chopped, keeping the whites and greens separate
3 teaspoons plain (all-purpose) flour
250g (9 oz/1 cup) crème fraîche
1 garlic clove, crushed
¼ teaspoon freshly grated nutmeg

CRUMBLE TOPPING
60 g (2¼ oz) butter
2½ tablespoons plain (all-purpose) flour
35 g (1¼ oz/⅓ cup) ground almonds
35 g (1¼ oz/⅓ cup) finely grated parmesan cheese
¼ teaspoon finely chopped rosemary

WHOLEMEAL PIROSHKI WITH LAMB AND EGGPLANT

SERVES 8

FILLING
1 tablespoon butter
1 tablespoon vegetable oil
1 brown onion, finely chopped
½ small eggplant (aubergine) (about 200 g/ 7 oz), cut into 1 cm (½ inch) dice
400 g (14 oz) minced (ground) lamb
2 garlic cloves, crushed
½ teaspoon ground allspice
1½ teaspoons ground cumin
½ teaspoon freshly grated nutmeg
1 bay leaf
80 ml (2½ fl oz/⅓ cup) vodka
250 ml (9 fl oz/1 cup) beef stock
2 teaspoons freshly squeezed lemon juice
1 handful coriander (cilantro) leaves or flat-leaf (Italian) parsley, finely chopped

To make the filling, heat the butter and oil in a saucepan over medium heat. Add the onion and eggplant and sauté for 10 minutes, or until the onion is lightly golden. Remove from the pan and set aside.

Add the lamb to the pan and brown well, breaking up any lumps with a fork. Add the garlic, allspice, cumin and nutmeg and cook for 1 minute further. Return the onion mixture to the pan and add the bay leaf, vodka, stock, lemon juice and 500 ml (17 fl oz/2 cups) water. Bring to the boil, then reduce the heat, cover and simmer for 1–1½ hours, or until the meat is very tender and the sauce has almost evaporated. Remove from the heat and season to taste. Cool slightly, stir in the coriander or parsley, then refrigerate until cold.

To make the dough, combine the yeast, sugar, 2 teaspoons of the plain flour and 60 ml (2 fl oz/¼ cup) of the warm milk in a non-metallic bowl. Cover with plastic wrap and set aside for 15 minutes, or until frothy. Stir in half the egg yolk and the melted butter. Into a separate bowl, sift together the remaining flours and ½ teaspoon salt, then tip in the husks from the sieve. Make a well in the centre of the flour and add the yeast mixture, then the sour cream and half of the remaining milk. Stir well to combine, adding a little more milk if needed, to form a fairly stiff dough. Turn out onto a lightly floured surface and knead for 10 minutes. Place the dough in a large greased bowl, turning to coat, then cover the bowl with plastic wrap. Set aside in a warm place (for example, near a warm oven) for 50–60 minutes or until doubled in size.

Preheat the oven to 200°C (400°F/Gas 6). Punch down the dough and roll out to a thickness of about 5 mm (¼ inch), then use an 8 cm (3¼ inch) pastry cutter to cut out eight individual rounds. Roll each round out as thinly as possible without tearing. Place 1½–2 tablespoons of the chilled lamb mixture in the centre of each dough round. Lightly brush the outside rim of one half of each circle with the egg white, then fold the opposite half over the top to form a crescent. Use a fork to press the edges together to seal.

Place the turnovers onto greased baking trays, spaced a good distance apart. Mix 1 tablespoon water into the remaining egg yolk and brush over the top of each turnover. Bake in the oven for about 25 minutes, or until golden. Serve hot on their own, or with yoghurt or sour cream dolloped on top.

Note: You can also deep-fry these turnovers if you prefer — simply cook the unglazed turnovers in a saucepan of oil heated to 180°C (350°F) for about 5 minutes, or until deep golden.

Variation: These turnovers can be filled with almost anything — savoury or sweet. Try quark (qvark) (see note, page 163) or ricotta with fruit or jam; mushrooms, dill and cream cheese; salmon, other seafood or chicken in a béchamel sauce; spinach, onion and cheese; or spiced bacon, cabbage, onion and potato; or make up your own delicious concoctions!

DOUGH

2 teaspoons active dried yeast
1 teaspoon caster (superfine) sugar
225 g (8 oz/1½ cups) plain (all-purpose) flour
125 ml (4 fl oz/½ cup) warm full-cream (whole) milk
4 egg yolks, lightly beaten
1½ tablespoons melted butter
150 g (5½ oz/1 cup) wholemeal (whole-wheat) flour
60 g (2¼ oz/¼ cup) sour cream
1 egg white, lightly beaten
Greek-style yoghurt or sour cream, to serve (optional)

FISH FRIKADELLER WITH CURRY REMOULADE

SERVES 6

To make the frikadeller, chill the bowl and blade of a food processor for a couple of hours. Meanwhile, remove any bones from the fish and roughly chop. Cover and chill. Working quickly, set up the food processor and process the fish, onion, cream, egg and egg white until a smooth paste is just formed. Add the breadcrumbs, flour, nutmeg, lemon zest, dill, white pepper and 1 teaspoon salt, and process again until well combined. Cover and refrigerate for 1 hour.

To make the remoulade, combine all of the ingredients and mix well. Cover and chill.

When ready to cook the frikadeller, heat a little of the butter and a good splash of oil in a large frying pan over medium heat. Use two spoons to carefully dollop a patty at a time into the pan, making sure they are well spaced. Flatten slightly and cook for about 2 minutes before turning. They should be lightly golden. Cook for a further 1–2 minutes, or until just cooked through. Drain the frikadeller on paper towels and eat straight away, when they're at their best, or keep them warm in a low oven while you cook the rest of the frikadeller — by adding a little more butter and oil to the pan and repeating the cooking process until all the mixture is used up.

Sprinkle the frikadeller with the chives and serve with lemon wedges and the remoulade on the side.

Note: Instead of frying the frikadeller, you can also poach balls of the mixture in a simmering, light seafood broth for a few minutes and then either drain and enjoy with the remoulade, or eat with the broth as a soup.

Variation: You can substitute fresh salmon for half of the white fish quantity if preferred.

500 g (1 lb 2 oz) fresh cod, perch or other firm white fish fillets
½ small white onion, grated and squeezed to extract excess moisture
185 ml (6 fl oz/¾ cup) pouring (whipping) cream, chilled
1 egg
1 egg white
40 g (1½ oz/½ cup) fresh white breadcrumbs
40 g (1½ oz/¼ cup) plain (all-purpose) flour
⅛ teaspoon freshly grated nutmeg
¼ teaspoon finely chopped lemon zest
1½ teaspoons finely chopped dill
a large pinch of white pepper
1 tablespoon butter
vegetable oil, for cooking
1 tablespoon finely snipped chives
lemon wedges, to serve

CURRY REMOULADE
125 g (4½ oz/½ cup) egg mayonnaise
1½ teaspoons Dijon mustard
1 small gherkin (pickle), finely chopped
1 anchovy, very finely chopped
1½ teaspoons freshly grated or bottled horseradish
½ teaspoon curry powder
½ teaspoon caster (superfine) sugar
1½ tablespoons finely snipped chives
1 teaspoon finely chopped dill

THREE-CHEESE POLENTA PIZZA WITH SWEET ONIONS AND WALNUTS

SERVES 4

1 tablespoon olive oil

2 teaspoons butter, plus 1 tablespoon extra

2 red onions, thinly sliced

125 ml (4 fl oz/½ cup) sweet Italian wine, such
   as Moscato or Vin santo

2 tablespoons caster (superfine) sugar

1 garlic clove, crushed

175 g (6 oz/1½ cups) instant polenta

150 g (5½ oz/1¼ cups) fontina cheese, grated

50 g (1¾ oz/½ cup) finely grated parmesan
   cheese

2 teaspoons small oregano leaves, plus extra,
   to garnish

40 g (1½ oz/⅓ cup) walnuts, chopped

75 g (2½ oz) gorgonzola or St Agur blue cheese,
   crumbled

Put the olive oil and butter in a small frying pan over medium heat. Add the onion and sauté for 15 minutes, or until lightly golden. Add the wine and sugar and bring to the boil. Reduce the heat and simmer for 5 minutes, or until the onion mixture is dark golden and caramelised, being careful that it doesn't burn. Remove from the heat and stir in the garlic.

Meanwhile, bring 685 ml (23½ fl oz/2¾ cups) water to the boil and gradually add the polenta, 1 teaspoon salt and the extra butter. Stir for 5 minutes, or until thick and creamy. Pour onto an oiled 30 cm (12 inch) pizza tray and spread out to an even thickness, about 1 cm (½ inch) thick. Allow to cool completely.

Preheat the oven to 200ºC (400ºF/Gas 6).

Spread the onion mixture over the cooled polenta, leaving a 1 cm (½ inch) border, then top with the combined fontina and parmesan cheeses. Scatter the oregano and walnuts over the top, then crumble on the blue cheese.

Place in the oven and cook for 20 minutes, or until the cheese is bubbling and lightly golden. Sprinkle over the extra oregano leaves. Serve immediately, in the pan.

Note: This recipe can also be made in four small pans for individual serves. A green salad of small peppery leaves with a sharp dressing would be a great side dish, as this pizza is quite rich.

SPICED WHEAT BEER AND BREAD SOUP WITH GARLIC CREAM

SERVES 6

Melt the butter in a large saucepan over medium heat. Add the onion and cook for 10 minutes or until lightly golden. Meanwhile, remove the crusts from the bread and cut into small dice.

Add the spices and bay leaves to the pan and cook for 1 minute, stirring often to release the flavours. Add the bread, beer, stock and sugar to the pan and bring to the boil, skimming any foam that rises to the surface. Reduce the heat and simmer for 40 minutes, or until the soup has thickened and the flavour is rich but mellow. Purée with a stick blender or in batches in a blender or a food processor. Season to taste.

While the soup is cooking, combine the sour cream, garlic and vinegar in a bowl and refrigerate until needed.

Serve the soup piping hot with a dollop of the garlic cream and some pumpernickel crumbs sprinkled on top.

Note: This soup thickens on standing. Add a little extra stock when reheating if necessary.

2 tablespoons butter

1 large brown onion, finely chopped

4 large slices dark pumpernickel bread

4 thick slices light rye bread

¼ teaspoon ground caraway

¼ teaspoon ground allspice

¼ teaspoon ground ginger

¼ teaspoon white pepper

2 bay leaves

375 ml (13 fl oz/1½ cups) wheat beer

1.5 litres (52 fl oz/6 cups) veal or beef stock

1 teaspoon soft brown sugar

1.5 litres (52 fl oz/6 cups) good-quality veal or beef stock

1 teaspoon soft brown sugar

GARLIC CREAM

165 g (5¾ oz/⅔ cup) sour cream

2 garlic cloves, crushed

1 tablespoon cider vinegar

1 large slice dark pumpernickel bread extra, crumbled

POLENTA LOAF WITH CHESTNUT, HONEY AND FENNEL BUTTER

SERVES 8

Preheat the oven to 170°C (325°F/Gas 3).

Place the figs, brandy and 1 tablespoon water in a small saucepan and bring to the boil. Turn off the heat and leave for 20 minutes, or until the figs have soaked up all the liquid. Cool, then roughly chop the figs.

Put the butter and honey into the bowl of an electric mixer and beat on high speed until pale and creamy. With the motor still running, beat in the egg yolks one at a time, mixing well after each addition. Use a spoon to mix in the chopped figs, zests, apple, pine nuts, ground almonds, flour, baking powder and polenta until well combined. Mix in the milk and vanilla until the batter is smooth. Whisk the egg whites to firm peaks and then beat 1 large spoonful into the batter. Gently fold in the rest of the egg white.

Spoon into a buttered 8 x 20 cm (3¼ x 8 inch) loaf (bar) tin and cook for 50 minutes, or until lightly golden on top and a skewer comes out clean when inserted into the centre of the loaf. Turn out onto a wire rack to cool slightly.

Meanwhile, make the butter by beating all the ingredients together until smooth. Spoon into a small dish.

Serve the loaf warm, cut into slices, with the butter and a drizzle of extra honey, if desired.

60 g (2¼ oz) dried figs
60 ml (2 fl oz/¼ cup) brandy
200 g (7 oz) unsalted butter
175 g (6 oz/½ cup) honey, plus extra, to serve
3 eggs, separated
1 teaspoon finely grated lemon zest
1 teaspoon finely grated orange zest
1 apple, peeled, cored and grated
50 g (1¾ oz/⅓ cup) pine nuts
55 g (2 oz/½ cup) ground almonds
100 g (3½ oz/⅔ cup) plain (all-purpose) flour, sifted
¼ teaspoon baking powder
150 g (5½ oz/1 cup) coarse-grain polenta
125 ml (4 fl oz/½ cup) full-cream (whole) milk
1 teaspoon natural vanilla extract

CHESTNUT, HONEY AND FENNEL BUTTER
125 g (4½ oz/½ cup) unsalted butter, softened
140 g (5 oz/½ cup) unsweetened chestnut purée
1 tablespoon honey
¾ teaspoon fennel seeds, toasted and ground

DOUGHNUT BALLS WITH MOCHA 'SOUP'

SERVES 6

15 g (½ oz) fresh yeast
185 ml (6 fl oz/¾ cup) warm full-cream
  (whole) milk
2 tablespoons caster (superfine) sugar
300 g (10½ oz/2 cups) plain (all-purpose) flour
1½ teaspoons ground cinnamon
2 egg yolks, lightly beaten
2½ tablespoons unsalted butter, melted
mild-flavoured vegetable oil, for deep-frying
vanilla sugar, for coating (see note)

MOCHA SOUP

1 litre (35 fl oz/4 cups) full-cream (whole) milk
2½ tablespoons sugar, or to taste
½ teaspoon natural vanilla extract
1 tablespoon strong espresso coffee,
  or to taste
1 tablespoon dark unsweetened cocoa powder
250 g (9 oz) dark chocolate, grated
6 large egg yolks, whisked
rum or vanilla vodka, to taste (optional)
chilled whipped cream and ground cinnamon
  or nutmeg, to serve (optional)

To make the doughnut balls, crumble the yeast into a small bowl and add 60 ml (2 fl oz/¼ cup) of the warm milk. Mash together to dissolve the yeast. Stir in 1 teaspoon of the sugar. Cover tightly with plastic wrap and set aside for 15 minutes, or until frothy.

Sift the flour, cinnamon and ¼ teaspoon salt into a large bowl. Stir in the remaining sugar and make a well in the centre. Pour the yeast mixture into the well, then add the egg yolks, melted butter and most of the remaining milk. Mix until a soft pliable dough is formed, adding a little more milk if needed.

Turn out onto a lightly floured surface and knead the dough for about 5 minutes, or until smooth. Place in a large bowl that has been greased with butter, and turn to coat the dough in the butter. Cover lightly with plastic wrap and set aside in a warm place (for example, near a warm oven) for 50–60 minutes, or until doubled in size.

Punch down the dough to flatten, then roll out into a rectangle about 1.5 cm (⅝ inch) thick. Use a 3 cm (1¼ inch) round pastry cutter and stamp out rounds, placing them onto a greased baking sheet — you should make about 30 rounds in total. Cover loosely with plastic wrap and rest for a further 10–15 minutes, or until slightly puffed.

While the doughnuts are resting, make the 'soup'. Set aside 2 tablespoons of the milk and put the rest in a saucepan with the sugar, vanilla, coffee and cocoa. Whisk over medium heat until the sugar has dissolved; do not allow to boil. Remove from the heat, add the chocolate and stir until almost melted. Beat the eggs yolks lightly with the reserved milk in a large bowl, then whisk in the hot milk mixture. Set aside.

Fill a deep-fryer or large heavy-based saucepan one-third full of oil and heat to 180°C (350°F), or until a cube of bread dropped into the oil browns in 15 seconds. Fry the doughnuts, in batches, for 2–3 minutes each, or until golden and puffed. Drain on paper towels, then roll in the vanilla sugar. Keep warm in a low oven while cooking the remaining doughnuts.

While the doughnuts are cooking, gently reheat the 'soup' over medium heat, stirring constantly for 10 minutes, or until it just comes to a simmer and thickens to a coating consistency. Stir in the rum or vodka if using, and pour into six cups. Serve with the hot doughnut balls, for dunking, and the whipped cream and ground cinnamon or nutmeg if desired.

Note: If you can't find vanilla sugar, it's quite easy to make your own. Simply put a vanilla bean in a jar filled with caster (superfine) sugar — the longer it sits in the sugar the more vanilla flavour the sugar will have. Keep it in your pantry for adding to recipes like this or stirring into hot drinks to sweeten.

Tip: These doughnuts are great without the chocolate soup as well — serve them in a basket accompanied by a selection of jams and compotes, or perhaps molasses for drizzling over.

SAFFRON AND CORIANDER SCROLLS WITH LEMON GLAZE

MAKES 16

Place the yeast, saffron and ⅓ cup of the warm milk in a non-metallic bowl and mash together to dissolve the yeast. Stir in the sugar and 2 teaspoons of the flour, cover tightly with plastic wrap and set aside for 15 minutes, or until frothy.

Mix together the egg, egg yolk and melted butter and stir into the yeast mixture. Sift the rest of the flour and ¼ teaspoon salt into a large bowl and make a well in the centre. Pour in the yeast mixture and most of the remaining milk and combine well, adding a little more milk if needed to make a pliable dough. Place in a large greased bowl and turn to coat. Cover lightly with plastic wrap and set aside in a warm place (for example, near a a warm oven) for 60 minutes, or until doubled in size.

Turn out onto a lightly floured surface and punch down the dough, then knead for 5 minutes, or until smooth and elastic and not sticky. Roll out to a large 50 x 50 cm (20 x 20 inch) square about 5 mm (¼ inch) thick. Spread the softened butter over the dough and sprinkle over the combined brown sugar, ground almonds, cinnamon and coriander. Roll up tightly like a swiss roll. Use a sharp knife to cut 3 cm (1¼ inch) thick slices and place the rounds flat on baking trays lined with baking paper — be sure to leave about 1.5 cm (⅝ inch) between the scrolls to allow for spreading. Cover with plastic wrap and set aside in a warm place for about 1 hour, or until doubled in size.

Meanwhile, preheat the oven to 200°C (400°F/Gas 6). Lightly beat the extra egg with 1 tablespoon of cold water, then brush over the tops of the buns. Bake in the oven for 15–20 minutes, or until golden. Remove the scrolls from the oven, place on a wire rack and cover with a clean tea towel (dish towel), for 5 minutes.

Meanwhile, make the lemon glaze by combining the icing sugar, lemon juice, vanilla and just enough water to make a smooth, slightly runny glaze. Drizzle half of the glaze over the scrolls and allow to cool for 10 minutes. Drizzle over the remaining glaze and allow to set. Enjoy with a piping hot cup of tea or coffee!

25 g (1 oz) fresh yeast

2 large pinches of saffron threads

250 ml (9 fl oz/1 cup) warm full-cream (whole) milk

2 tablespoons caster (superfine) sugar

525 g (1 lb 2½ oz/3½ cups) plain (all-purpose) flour

1 egg, plus 1 extra, for glazing

1 egg yolk

2 tablespoons unsalted butter, melted

165 g (5¾ oz) unsalted butter, softened

95 g (3¼ oz/½ cup) soft brown sugar

2 tablespoons ground almonds

1 tablespoon ground cinnamon

1½ tablespoons ground coriander

LEMON GLAZE

125 g (4½ oz/1 cup) icing (confectioners') sugar, sifted

2 tablespoons freshly squeezed lemon juice

½ teaspoon natural vanilla extract

PANETTONE, CHOCOLATE AND MARSHMALLOW MELTS

MAKES 8

1 large panettone, cut into eight 1 cm
  (½ inch) thick slices
100 g (3½ oz) unsalted butter, softened
Amaretto for sprinkling
2 x 100 g (3½ oz) thin blocks of dark chocolate
  (70% cocoa)
12 white marshmallows, cut in half
30 g (1 oz/¼ cup) icing (confectioners')
  sugar
1 teaspoon ground cinnamon

Trim the edges of each slice of panettone so that you have eight neat 10 x 10 cm (4 x 4 inch) squares. Cut each square in half to form sixteen smaller 5 x 10 cm (2 x 4 inch) rectangles. Liberally butter one side of each piece.

Lay a piece of plastic wrap on a clean work surface and place eight panettone slices, buttered side down, on the wrap. Sprinkle a little Amaretto over the top. Use a very sharp knife dipped in hot water and cut each block of the chocolate into four wide strips; lay one piece on each of the panettone fingers, then add three marshmallow pieces along the length of the chocolate. Top with another piece of the panettone, buttered side up, to make a 'sandwich'. You should end up with eight small sandwiches in total.

Heat a large frying pan over medium heat. Carefully lift up each sandwich, holding them together to make sure the filling doesn't fall out and cook for 2–3 minutes on one side, before carefully turning over and cooking the other side for 2–3 minutes, or until both the chocolate and marshmallows have melted and the panettone is golden and crisp. Remove from the pan and place on a serving platter.

Mix the icing sugar and cinnamon together and sift over the hot sandwiches. Serve immediately.

RAISIN ALE CAKE WITH WALNUT STREUSEL TOPPING

SERVES 8

Put the raisins in a bowl and pour over enough boiling water to cover. Rest for 20 minutes or until plump. Drain well and roughly chop.

Make the streusel topping by combining all the ingredients and mixing well. Preheat the oven to 170°C (325°F/Gas 3).

Put the butter, sour cream, sugar, cardamom and lemon zest in the bowl of an electric mixer and beat on high speed until pale and creamy. With the motor still running, beat in the eggs, one at a time, mixing well after each addition. Mix in the vanilla and raisins. Sift the flour and baking powder together in a separate bowl. Fold half the flour mixture into the butter mixture, then add half of the beer and mix well to combine. Repeat with the remaining flour mixture and beer until well combined. Spoon the mixture into a 23 cm (9 inch) round non-stick spring-form cake tin and evenly sprinkle over the streusel topping.

Bake on the middle shelf of the oven for 50–55 minutes, or until a skewer comes out clean when inserted into the centre of the cake. Remove from the oven and cool slightly in the tin, then remove from the tin and cool for a few minutes more on a wire rack. Serve warm or at room temperature.

Note: This cake is great served with ice cream or whipped cream flavoured with a little ground cardamom and sweetened to taste, or simply spread with butter.

85 g (3 oz/⅔ cup) raisins
150 g (5½ oz) unsalted butter, softened
125 g (4½ oz/½ cup) sour cream
170 g (6 oz/¾ cup) caster (superfine) sugar
½ teaspoon ground cardamom
1 teaspoon finely grated lemon zest
3 large eggs, at room temperature
1 teaspoon natural vanilla extract
375 g (13 oz/2½ cups) plain (all-purpose) flour, sifted
½ teaspoon baking powder
170 ml (5½ fl oz/⅔ cup) pale ale, at room temperature
whipped cream or ice cream, to serve

STREUSEL TOPPING
100 g (3½ oz) unsalted butter, softened
125 g (4½ oz/⅔ cup) soft brown sugar
90 g (3¼ oz/¾ cup) roughly chopped walnuts
60 g (2¼ oz) marzipan, chopped, optional
50 g (1¾ oz/⅓ cup) plain (all-purpose) flour

MULLED WINE

SERVES 8

1 orange, sliced
¼ teaspoon ground cardamom
½ teaspoon ground coriander
1 teaspoon ground cinnamon
½ teaspoon ground fennel
½ teaspoon ground ginger
3 cloves
60 g (2¼ oz/½ cup) slivered almonds, optional
40 g (1½ oz/⅓ cup) raisins, optional
750 ml (26 fl oz/3 cups) red wine
250 ml (9 fl oz/1 cup) port
2 tablespoons sugar
125 ml (4 fl oz/½ cup) Akvavit (Aquavit)
  (see note, page 29)
cinnamon sticks, to serve (optional)

Put 750 ml (26 fl oz/3 cups) water in a saucepan with the orange slices, cardamom, coriander, cinnamon, fennel, ginger and cloves. Bring to the boil, then reduce the heat and simmer for 5 minutes. Add the almonds and raisins, if using. Remove from the heat and set aside for 15 minutes for the flavours to infuse.

Strain into a clean saucepan, add the wine, port and sugar, and stir over medium heat until the sugar has dissolved; do not allow it to boil. Add the Akvavit and pour into cups or heatproof glasses. Serve with long spoons for eating the almonds and raisins, if using. Cinnamon sticks can be added to the cups to intensify the aroma.

Note: For a non-alcoholic version of this mulled wine, replace the wine and port with grape juice or blackcurrant juice cordial made up in accordance with the manufacturer's directions.

CHERRY MINT WARMER

SERVES 4

Put the cherry juice, peppermint and cherries in a saucepan and slowly bring to the boil over a medium–high heat. Reduce the heat and simmer for 5 minutes. Remove from the heat and set aside for 20 minutes to allow the flavours to infuse. Bring to the boil again over high heat. Remove from the heat. Discard the peppermint and allow to cool for 1 minute, then stir in the schnapps and Kirsch. Pour into heatproof glasses and serve with a spoon or fork to eat the cherries.

1 litre (35 fl oz/4 cups) bottled cherry juice
½ teaspoon dried peppermint, tied in muslin (cheesecloth)
2 tablespoons dried sour cherries
80 ml (2½ fl oz/⅓ cup) sweet dark cherry schnapps or liqueur
80 ml (2½ fl oz/⅓ cup) Kirsch

WARM APPLE TODDY

SERVES 6

750 ml (26 fl oz/3 cups) clear apple juice
½ teaspoon freshly grated nutmeg
1½ teaspoons allspice berries
1 small apple, thinly sliced
500 ml (17 fl oz/2 cups) sparkling apple cider
80 ml (2½ fl oz/⅓ cup) Calvados

Put the apple juice, nutmeg and allspice berries in a saucepan and bring to the boil. Remove from the heat and set aside for 15 minutes to allow the flavours to infuse, then place back over high heat and bring just to the boil again.

Meanwhile, put the apple slices into the base of a large pitcher. Strain the hot apple juice over the top, then stir in the apple cider and Calvados and serve.

BUTTERED BALSAM

SERVES 4

Divide the Balsam between four heatproof glasses or mugs. Put a strip of orange zest into each glass and sprinkle with a tiny pinch of cloves. Top up with water that has recently boiled, but has cooled very slightly. Add a teaspoon of butter to the top of each and serve with brown sugar to taste.

Note: Riga Black Balsam is a traditional Latvian herbal liqueur made from natural ingredients and mixed with vodka.

200 ml (7 fl oz) Riga Black Balsam (see note) or dark rum
4 strips orange zest, white pith removed
a pinch of ground cloves
4 teaspoons butter
soft brown sugar, to taste

GINGERBREAD–SPICE COFFEE

SERVES 4

25 g (1 oz/⅓ cup) finely ground coffee, suitable for a plunger
1 teaspoon ground cinnamon
¼ teaspoon ground coriander
½ teaspoon ground ginger
a small pinch of cloves
3 teaspoons molasses, or to taste
½ teaspoon natural vanilla extract
4 cinnamon sticks, to serve
milk or pouring (whipping) cream, to serve
soft brown sugar, to serve

Put the coffee and spices into a 1 litre (35 fl oz/4 cup) coffee plunger and half-fill the plunger with boiling water. Stir in the molasses and vanilla and then continue to fill the plunger to the level mark with boiling water. Plunge after 3 minutes.

Divide the cinnamon sticks between four large heatproof glasses or mugs, then pour in the coffee. Serve with milk or cream and sugar for guests to add as they like.

ALMOND HOT CHOCOLATE

SERVES 4

Whip the cream to firm peaks and fold through the marshmallow. Cover and refrigerate until ready to use.

Grate or finely chop the chocolate and put in a heatproof bowl.

Put the milk, vanilla, almond extract and cocoa in a saucepan and, stirring occasionally, bring almost to the boil. Reduce the heat and simmer for 3 minutes. Strain through a fine sieve onto the chocolate and whisk until as smooth as possible and the colour is consistent. Place back over a gentle heat and bring just to a simmer again.

Pour into four large heatproof glasses or mugs and top with the whipped marshmallow cream. Sprinkle with the cinnamon and top with the flaked almonds. Serve immediately with sugar on the side for people to sweeten as they like.

Note: Try adding a splash of chocolate, almond liqueur, or rum just before serving for something a little more decadent!

125 ml (4 fl oz/½ cup) pouring (whipping) cream
12 marshmallows, very finely chopped
400g (14 oz) dark chocolate (70% cocoa)
875 ml (30 fl oz/3½ cups) full-cream (whole) milk
½ teaspoon natural vanilla extract
¼ teaspoon natural almond extract, or to taste
1 teaspoon good-quality unsweetened cocoa powder
ground cinnamon, for sprinkling
flaked almonds, to serve
sugar, to taste

ELDERFLOWER, GIN AND LEMON SIPPER

SERVES 4

125 ml (4 fl oz/½ cup) elderflower cordial
1 teaspoon freshly squeezed lemon juice
4 long strips of lemon zest
dried elderflowers or chamomile flowers
   (optional)
170 ml (5½ fl oz/⅔ cup) gin

Combine the elderflower cordial and lemon juice and divide between four heatproof glasses. Place a strip of zest and a small sprig of dried elderflowers or a few dried chamomile flowers, if using, into each glass. Pour in enough boiling water to fill the glass about two-thirds full and stir well. Rest for 1 minute, then divide the gin between the glasses.

Note: Of course you can also leave out the gin for a refreshing non-alcoholic drink.

HONEY AND SAFFRON LIQUEUR

MAKES ABOUT 1 LITRE

Put the honey, 125 ml (4 fl oz/½ cup) water, the vanilla bean, cinnamon stick, peppercorns, allspice, nutmeg and saffron in a saucepan and bring just to the boil. Quickly reduce the heat and simmer for 5 minutes. Remove from the heat, add the lemon zest and set aside to infuse for 20 minutes. Reheat until simmering, then remove from the heat, cool completely, strain, then stir in the vodka. Carefully pour into a sterilised airtight bottle and allow to steep for a week. Serve chilled or slightly warmed.

350 g (12 oz/1 cup) honey
½ vanilla bean, finely chopped
1 cinnamon stick
10 white peppercorns
6 allspice berries
¼ teaspoon freshly grated nutmeg
a small pinch of saffron threads
3 strips of lemon zest, white pith removed
750 ml (26 fl oz/3 cups) Polish vodka

WARMED TO THE CORE

WHETHER COCOONED IN WOOL AND ABOUT TO BRAVE THE ELEMENTS OR
HIBERNATING IN AN OVERSIZED ARMCHAIR HIDING FROM THE FREEZE,
YOU WILL TAKE COMFORT FROM THESE BREAKFASTS AND ENJOY
THE SUSTENANCE OF THESE SIMMERING, SLOW-COOKED RECIPES.
PARTAKE IN A NOURISHING MEAL DESIGNED TO SOFTEN THE BLOW
OF THE CHILLY SPELL AND FUEL YOURSELF FOR THE HOURS AHEAD.

CREAMED POLENTA WITH CINNAMON PRUNES

SERVES 4–6

CINNAMON PRUNES
20 pitted prunes
1 cinnamon stick
a small pinch of ground cloves
2 tablespoons caster (superfine) sugar
1 tablespoon honey

1 vanilla bean, split
500 ml (17 fl oz/2 cups) full-cream (whole) milk
1 wide strip lemon zest, white pith removed
100 g (3½ oz/⅔ cup) instant fine polenta
4 tablespoons caster (superfine) sugar
125 ml (4 fl oz/½ cup) pouring (whipping)
  cream, plus extra, to serve
30 g (1 oz/¼ cup) hazelnuts, roasted
  and chopped

Put the prunes, cinnamon stick, cloves, sugar and honey in a saucepan with 310 ml (10¾ fl oz/1¼ cups) water. Stir over medium–high heat until the sugar has dissolved and bring to the boil. Reduce to a simmer and cook for 10 minutes, or until the prunes are very soft but not falling apart. Remove the prunes to a plate. Bring the liquid to the boil and cook over high heat for 5 minutes or until syrupy. Return the prunes to the pan. Cover and set aside.

Scrape the seeds of the vanilla bean into a large saucepan and add the bean, along with the milk, lemon zest and 500 ml (17 fl oz/2 cups) water. Bring almost to the boil over a medium–high heat, then reduce to a simmer. Gradually add the polenta, stirring constantly. Continue to stir for 10–15 minutes, or until thickened and creamy — the mixture should be smooth and not at all gritty. Add the sugar and cream and cook for a further 5 minutes, or until the sugar has dissolved.

Divide the polenta between four or six bowls, top with the prunes and drizzle over the remaining syrup. Scatter over some hazelnuts and serve immediately with extra cream for pouring over, if you desire, or perhaps some mascarpone.

Variation: For a different take on this dish, try using dates in place of the prunes. It tastes just as good!

SPICED BUTTERMILK WAFFLES WITH RHUBARB MOLASSES AND ORANGE WHIPPED BUTTER

SERVES 4

To make the rhubarb molasses, put all the ingredients into a small saucepan over high heat and bring to the boil. Reduce the heat and simmer for 5 minutes, or until the rhubarb is very tender. Strain the liquid into a bowl and discard the solids. Return the liquid to the pan and simmer, stirring for 3–4 minutes, until sticky.

To make the orange whipped butter, combine the softened butter with the orange zest and sugar in a bowl and beat with electric beaters for 10 minutes, or until pale and creamy. Set aside. Refrigerate if your room is warm, or you are making the butter in advance, but whip again just before you intend to serve.

To make the waffles, sift the flour, baking powder and spices into a bowl. Stir in the sugar and make a well in the centre. Whisk together the buttermilk and egg yolks in a separate bowl and pour into the well. Continue whisking the mixture until smooth and the consistency of thin custard, adding more buttermilk if necessary. Set aside for 10 minutes. Whisk the egg whites with a pinch of salt until firm peaks form. Mix a spoonful of the whites into the batter, then fold through the rest.

Heat a waffle iron or electric waffle maker according to the manufacturer's instructions and brush with a little melted butter. Ladle one-quarter to one-third of a cup into the centre and close the lid. Cook for 8 minutes or until golden. Remove from the waffle iron and place on a wire rack in a low oven to keep warm while you use up the remaining waffle batter — you should make eight waffles in total.

Serve the hot waffles with a dollop of the orange-whipped butter on top and drizzle with the rhubarb molasses.

Note: If you don't have time to make the rhubarb molasses and the whipped butter, then a good-quality plain butter or whipped cream and lingonberry jam, or perhaps some maple syrup, make great substitutes.

RHUBARB MOLASSES

3 rhubarb stems, finely chopped
80 ml (2½ fl oz/⅓ cup) freshly squeezed orange juice, strained
3 teaspoons molasses
55 g (2 oz/¼ cup) caster (superfine) sugar
1 teaspoon natural vanilla extract

ORANGE WHIPPED BUTTER

80 g (2¾ oz) unsalted butter, softened
1½ teaspoons finely grated orange zest
1 teaspoon soft brown sugar

WAFFLES

225 g (8 oz/1½ cups) plain (all-purpose) flour
¼ teaspoon baking powder
1 teaspoon ground cinnamon
½ teaspoon ground cardamom
½ teaspoon ground ginger
2 tablespoons caster (superfine) sugar
310 ml (10¾ fl oz/1¼ cups) buttermilk
2 eggs, separated
melted butter, for cooking

BIRCHER MUESLI PANCAKES WITH CRANBERRY APPLE COMPOTE AND YOGHURT

SERVES 4-6

MUESLI PANCAKES

100 g (3½ oz/1 cup) rolled (porridge) oats

2 tablespoons sunflower seeds

1½ tablespoons rye or bran flakes

2 tablespoons dried cranberries

40 g (1½ oz/¼ cup) chopped raw almonds

310 ml (10¾ fl oz/1¼ cups) full-cream (whole) milk

40 g (1½ oz/¼ cup) plain (all-purpose) flour

1½ teaspoons baking powder

1 teaspoon ground cinnamon

1 tablespoon soft brown sugar

2 large eggs

melted butter, for cooking

Greek-style or vanilla yoghurt, to serve

CRANBERRY APPLE COMPOTE

125 g (4½ oz/1 cup) frozen cranberries

1 apple, cored and diced

125 ml (4 fl oz/½ cup) cranberry juice

1 teaspoon natural vanilla extract

½ teaspoon finely grated orange zest

55 g (2 oz/¼ cup) caster (superfine) sugar

½ tablespoon honey

To make the muesli pancakes, put the rolled oats, sunflower seeds, rye or bran flakes, cranberries, almonds and milk in a bowl and mix well. Cover and refrigerate overnight.

To make the cranberry apple compote, place all of the ingredients in a saucepan and stir over high heat until the sugar has dissolved. Bring to the boil, then reduce the heat and simmer for 15 minutes, or until the fruit is tender and the sauce has thickened slightly. Either keep warm if making pancakes straight away or gently reheat when ready to serve.

When ready to cook the pancakes, add the flour, baking powder, cinnamon, sugar and eggs to the muesli mixture and combine thoroughly. Set aside for 10 minutes.

Brush a little melted butter in a large non-stick frying pan over medium heat. Cook the pancakes in batches, using 60 ml (2 fl oz/¼ cup) of mixture for each pancake — you should make eight small pancakes in total. Cook the pancakes on each side for 3 minutes, or until lightly golden and cooked through. Serve pancakes topped with the cranberry and apple compote and a dollop of yoghurt.

BACON ROSTI WITH POACHED EGGS AND THYME HOLLANDAISE

SERVES 4

BACON ROSTI

4 waxy or all-purpose potatoes (about
  750 g/1 lb 10 oz), washed but not peeled
2 tablespoons butter
1 streaky bacon slice, finely chopped
1 small brown onion, finely chopped
1 thyme sprig, leaves very finely chopped
1 handful chives, snipped
vegetable oil, for cooking

THYME HOLLANDAISE

2 egg yolks
1 tablespoon freshly squeezed lemon juice
1 small thyme sprig, leaves finely chopped
a small pinch of white pepper
100 g (3½ oz) butter, cut into 1 cm
  (½ inch) cubes

4 large eggs
1 tablespoon vinegar

Cook the potatoes in a large saucepan of boiling water for 10–12 minutes, or until just starting to become tender but still firm in the centre.

Make the hollandaise while the potatoes are cooking. Put the egg yolks, lemon juice, thyme and white pepper in a small bowl and whisk to combine. Place the bowl over a saucepan of simmering water and whisk constantly for 8 minutes, or until thickened slightly. Add the butter, 2–3 cubes at a time, whisking constantly. Don't add any more butter until each addition has been incorporated and remember to keep whisking so the sauce doesn't separate. When all the butter is added you should have a smooth glossy sauce. Remove from the heat and cover to keep warm.

Drain and cool the potatoes completely, then peel and discard the skin and coarsely grate the potatoes into a bowl. Heat the butter in a small frying pan over medium heat. Add the bacon and onion and cook for 5 minutes, or until the onion is lightly golden. Add to the potatoes with the thyme and two-thirds of the chives. Season well and combine thoroughly.

Heat a little oil in a non-stick frying pan over medium–high heat and add a quarter of the potato mixture. Press down with a spatula until about 1.5 cm (⅝ inch) thick all over. Cook for 5 minutes, or until golden on the bottom, then carefully turn over and cook on the other side for 5 minutes, or until golden. Drain on paper towels and keep warm on a baking tray in a low oven while you cook the remaining mixture, adding a little extra oil as needed to make four röstis in total.

Half-fill a large, deep frying pan with water and bring to the boil. Reduce to a simmer and add the vinegar. Carefully crack each egg into a teacup. Use a wooden spoon to stir the water in the pan until you have a whirlpool effect, then quickly but carefully slide the eggs from each cup into the water at intervals so they are as evenly spaced around the pan as can be. Cover and cook for 2–3 minutes, depending on how firm you like your yolks. If you don't feel confident to cook all the eggs at once, as it can take some practice, just cook one or two at a time. You can also pan-fry the eggs in a little butter if you prefer.

Gently reheat the hollandaise. Top each rösti with an egg and a dollop of hollandaise, and garnish with the remaining snipped chives.

Variation: You can add a little wilted spinach or silverbeet (swiss chard) that has been tossed with butter and nutmeg over the rösti before topping with the egg and hollandaise. Rösti can also be served plain, on their own or as a side dish. Adding some grated apple to the potato mixture makes them perfect for accompanying pork mains.

SAVOURY BUCKWHEAT KASHA WITH DILLED MUSHROOMS

SERVES 6

1½ tablespoons dried porcini (cep) mushroom slices
1.5 litres (52 fl oz/6 cups) light chicken stock or water
2½ tablespoons butter
350 g (12 oz/2 cups) cracked buckwheat
½ small onion, finely chopped
500 g (1 lb 2 oz) field mushrooms, sliced
160 g (5¾ oz/⅔ cup) sour cream
1 garlic clove, crushed
1 handful dill, chopped

Crumble the porcini slices into a saucepan. Add the stock or water and slowly bring to the boil. Remove from the heat and set aside.

Melt ½ tablespoon of the butter in a large, deep-sided frying pan over medium–high heat and add the buckwheat, stirring constantly for 5 minutes, or until slightly golden and aromatic.

Strain the porcini soaking liquid, reserving the rehydrated mushrooms, and gradually stir the liquid into the buckwheat. Bring to the boil, then reduce the heat, cover, and simmer for 20 minutes, stirring occasionally, until the buckwheat is very tender and almost all the liquid has been absorbed. Season to taste.

Meanwhile, prepare the dilled mushrooms. Finely chop the rehydrated porcini. Melt the remaining butter in a saucepan over medium heat. Add the onion and sauté for 5 minutes, or until lightly golden then add the porcini and field mushrooms and cook for 10 minutes, or until softened and any liquid released has evaporated. Remove from the heat, stir in the sour cream, garlic and dill, and season to taste.

Divide the buckwheat between four bowls and top with the mushroom mixture. Serve immediately.

Variation: Kasha can also be served sweet — simply cook the buckwheat in water and serve with milk, cream or butter and some honey or jam.

PORK AND CABBAGE CAKES WITH SWEET ONION RELISH

SERVES 4–6

To make the pork and cabbage cakes combine all the ingredients in a non-metallic bowl and mix with clean hands until very well combined. Cover tightly and refrigerate overnight for the flavours to combine.

To make the relish, heat the butter and oil in a saucepan over medium heat. Add the onions and cook for 10 minutes, stirring occasionally, until lightly golden. Add the remaining ingredients, ½ teaspoon salt and 500 ml (17 fl oz/2 cups) water and bring to the boil. Reduce the heat and simmer for 30–40 minutes, stirring occasionally, until most of the liquid has evaporated. Remove from the heat and cover to keep warm while you cook the pork and cabbage cakes.

Remove the pork and cabbage mixture from the refrigerator and season well. Divide the mixture into eight even portions. Using your hands, roll each portion into a ball and flatten slightly to make patties about 1.5 cm (⅝ inch) thick. Lightly grease a large non-stick frying pan and place over medium heat. Cook the patties for 4 minutes on each side, or until lightly golden. Serve the patties with the sweet onion relish.

Variation: Top the patties with poached or fried eggs before spooning over the relish, or add some crispy bacon and seared apple slices.

PORK AND CABBAGE CAKES

400 g (14 oz) minced (ground) pork
1 streaky bacon slice, finely chopped
½ small brown onion, finely chopped
150 g (5½ oz/2 cups) finely shredded green cabbage
200 g (7 oz/2½ cups) fresh white breadcrumbs
1 large egg
⅛ teaspoon white pepper
½ teaspoon finely chopped marjoram
1 garlic clove, crushed
½ teaspoon finely grated lemon zest
¼ teaspoon finely grated fresh nutmeg
⅛ teaspoon ground allspice

SWEET ONION RELISH

1 tablespoon butter
1 tablespoon sunflower oil
2 brown onions, chopped
1 tablespoon yellow mustard seeds
1 bay leaf
¼ teaspoon Hungarian hot paprika
a small pinch of ground cloves
125 ml (4 fl oz/½ cup) cider vinegar
3 tablespoons soft brown sugar

ITALIAN-STYLE MEATLOAF WITH LENTILS

SERVES 6

MEATLOAF
240 g (8¾ oz/3 cups) fresh white breadcrumbs
125 ml (4 fl oz/½ cup) pouring (whipping) cream
500 g (1 lb 2 oz) minced (ground) veal
500 g (1 lb 2 oz) minced (ground) pork
1 brown onion, very finely chopped
1 teaspoon finely grated lemon zest
4 anchovies, very finely chopped
2 tablespoons capers in vinegar, drained and
    finely chopped
3 garlic cloves, crushed
1 teaspoon freshly ground nutmeg
1½ tablespoons chopped sage
1 large handful flat-leaf (Italian) parsley,
    finely chopped
2 large eggs, beaten

LENTILS
1 tablespoon butter
50 g (1¾ oz) pancetta, finely chopped
1 small brown onion, finely chopped
1 carrot, finely diced
1 celery stalk, finely diced
1 bay leaf
60 ml (2 fl oz/¼ cup) white wine
750 g (1 lb 10 oz/4 cups) lightly cooked brown
    or green lentils
170 ml (5½ fl oz/⅔ cup) good-quality
    veal stock
aged balsamic glaze, to taste (see note)
    (optional)
1 large handful flat-leaf (Italian) parsley,
    roughly chopped

To make the meatloaf, combine the breadcrumbs and cream and set aside. Put the veal and pork mince in a non-metallic bowl with the onion, lemon zest, anchovies, capers, garlic, nutmeg, sage and parsley and mix well. Add the soaked breadcrumbs and the egg, and mix thoroughly, using clean hands. Really get in there! Cover tightly and refrigerate for at least 6 hours or overnight.

Preheat the oven to 170°C (325°F/Gas 3). Line the base of a 24 x 14 x 7 cm (9½ x 5½ x 2¾ inch) loaf (bar) tin with baking paper. Lightly grease the tin, spoon in the meatloaf mixture and smooth over the top with wet hands. Cover tightly with foil. Cook the meatloaf for 40 minutes, then remove the foil and cook for a further 40 minutes, or until firm to the touch and the top is lightly golden — the meatloaf should start to come away from the edge of the tin. Remove from the oven, cover and set aside to rest for 10–15 minutes.

Meanwhile, prepare the lentils. Melt the butter in a saucepan over medium–high heat. Add the pancetta, onion, carrot, celery and bay leaf and cook for 10 minutes, or until the onion is lightly golden. Add the wine, bring to the boil and cook for 1 minute. Add the lentils and stock and stir to combine. Bring to the boil, then reduce the heat and simmer for 10 minutes, or until the lentils are tender and heated through. Season, drizzle with a little balsamic, if using, to taste, and stir through the parsley.

Invert the meatloaf onto a board, cut the very ends off to neaten, then cut into six thick slices. Divide the lentils between six plates, top with a slice of the meatloaf and serve immediately.

Notes: You can buy cooked lentils in a tin or cook dried lentils in boiling water until just starting to become tender — the time will vary depending on the lentils used.

Balsamic glaze is thickened, sweet balsamic and is available at good delicatessens.

ONE POT LAMB AND CABBAGE

SERVES 6–8

Preheat the oven to 180°C (350°F/Gas 4). Heat the oil and butter in a large frying pan over medium–high heat. Season the lamb chops with salt and freshly cracked black pepper and brown well on each side. Remove from the pan and set aside.

Divide the cabbage into three equal portions. Line the base of a large, deep baking dish or roasting tin with one portion of the cabbage, then scatter over half the onion. Make another layer with half of the potato and kohlrabi, then place half the chops in a single layer on top. Sprinkle with lightly ground cloves, half of the thyme and 1 bay leaf. Repeat this layering and finish with the final portion of cabbage. Sprinkle the bacon on top. Combine the vinegar, stock and beer and carefully pour over.

Cover with foil and cook for 2 hours, carefully lifting the foil and pressing the layers into the braising liquid occasionally. Remove the foil and cook for a further 30–45 minutes, or until the lamb is very tender.

Variation: You can use pork chops instead of lamb chops if you prefer.

2 tablespoons vegetable oil

1 tablespoon butter

2 kg (4 lb 8 oz) lamb shoulder chops

1.5 kg (3 lb 5 oz/½ large head) green cabbage, sliced

2 brown onions, thinly sliced

2 large all-purpose potatoes, such as desiree, peeled and thinly sliced

1 kohlrabi (bout 400 g/14 oz), peeled and thinly sliced

ground cloves, for sprinkling

1 large thyme sprig, leaves finely chopped

2 fresh bay leaves, crumbled

3 streaky bacon slices, finely chopped

80 ml (2½ fl oz/⅓ cup) white wine vinegar

435 ml (15¼ fl oz/1¾ cups) chicken stock

125 ml (4 fl oz/½ cup) pale ale beer

BEER, ORANGE AND SPICE BRAISED SHORT RIBS WITH WALNUT DUMPLINGS

SERVES 6

2 tablespoons vegetable oil
2 tablespoons butter
1 large brown onion, chopped
2 carrots, diced
1 parsnip or small swede (rutabaga), diced
1 celery stalk, diced
1 bay leaf
2 tablespoons plain (all-purpose) flour
2 kg (4 lb 8 oz) beef short ribs
2 garlic cloves, crushed
1 teaspoon ground cinnamon
1 teaspoon ground coriander
½ teaspoon ground ginger
1½ teaspoons finely grated orange zest
170 ml (5½ fl oz/⅔ cup) freshly squeezed orange juice, strained
375 ml (13 fl oz/1½ cups) wheat beer
500 ml (17 fl oz/2 cups) beef stock

WALNUT DUMPLINGS
185 ml (6 fl oz/¾ cup) full-cream (whole) milk
1 egg
40 g (1½ oz) butter, melted
190 g (6¾ oz/1¼ cups) plain (all-purpose) flour
30 g (1 oz/¼ cup) potato flour
2 teaspoons baking powder
1 teaspoon finely grated orange zest
3 tablespoons roasted walnuts, chopped
1 handful flat-leaf (Italian) parsley, finely chopped

Heat half of the oil and butter in a large flameproof casserole dish over medium heat. Add the onion, carrot, parsnip, celery and bay leaf and cook for 10 minutes, stirring occasionally, until lightly golden. Remove the vegetables from the dish and set aside. Add the remaining oil and butter to the dish. Season the flour with salt and freshly ground black pepper and toss with the short ribs to lightly coat. Lightly brown the ribs, in batches, and set aside with the vegetables.

Add the garlic, spices, orange zest and juice, beer, stock and 375 ml (13 fl oz/1½ cups) water to the casserole dish and stir, scraping up any cooked-on bits. Return the vegetable mixture and the ribs to the dish and stir to combine. Bring to the boil over high heat, then reduce the heat, cover, and simmer for 1 hour 20 minutes. Uncover and cook for a further 40 minutes, or until the sauce has thickened slightly.

Preheat the oven to 180°C (350°F/Gas 4).

Meanwhile, make the dumplings by combining the milk, egg and butter in a large bowl. Sift in the combined flours and baking powder along with the orange zest, walnuts, parsley and 1 teaspoon salt, mixing until just combined. Roll tablespoons of the mixture into balls and add to the casserole. Bake in the oven for a further 30 minutes, or until the dumplings are golden and cooked through and the ribs are very tender.

Serve the ribs and dumplings in the casserole dish at the table so that people can help themselves.

ALMOND-CRUSTED SCHNITZEL WITH PICKLED CABBAGE

SERVES 6

Finely shred the cabbage and spread half into a very large non-metallic baking dish or deep-sided plastic tray. Sprinkle with the sea salt, then cover with the remaining cabbage. Using very clean hands, mulch it together to bruise the cabbage with the salt. Keep mulching until the salt has dissolved in the liquid that is released. Lightly crumple the bay leaves and add to the cabbage with the caraway seeds and juniper berries and mix through. Pack the mixture down firmly with your hands, then cover tightly with plastic wrap. Refrigerate for 24 hours, mixing occasionally with clean hands or a wooden spoon and resealing each time.

Using a meat mallet, beat the schnitzel pieces as thin as possible without tearing — about 3 mm (⅛ inch). Combine the buttermilk, garlic, sage and mustard in a shallow, non-metallic baking dish. Add the schnitzel pieces and turn to coat in the mixture. Seal with plastic wrap and marinate in the refrigerator for 4–6 hours. Remove from the marinade and allow any excess liquid to drip off. Lightly coat each schnitzel piece in seasoned flour, then dip into the egg. Allow any excess to drip off, then coat in the combined breadcrumbs and ground almonds. Press down to help adhere. Refrigerate until ready to cook.

When ready to cook the cabbage, rinse well and discard the bay leaves and juniper berries. Squeeze out any excess moisture from the cabbage. Heat the oil and butter in a large frying pan over medium heat. Add the onion and cook for 5 minutes, stirring occasionally, until lightly golden. Add the cabbage, apple and wine and stir to combine. Reduce the heat to low and cook for 20 minutes, stirring occasionally, until the wine has been cooked out and the cabbage is heated through. Stir through the vinegar and cook for a further 5 minutes. Season with salt, to taste.

Meanwhile, to cook the schnitzel pieces, heat 1 cm (½ inch) oil in a large heavy-based frying pan over medium heat. Cook the schnitzels, in batches, for 3 minutes on each side, or until golden and cooked through. Drain on paper towels, season lightly, and serve hot with the cabbage and lemon wedges on the side for squeezing over.

Tip: Potato salad or steamed vegetables make nice accompaniments to this schnitzel dish.

1.5 kg (3 lb 12 oz, about ½ large head) green cabbage
2 tablespoons sea salt or kosher salt
4 bay leaves
2 teaspoons caraway seeds
2 teaspoons juniper berries, lightly crushed
1 tablespoon vegetable oil
1 tablespoon butter
1 brown onion, thinly sliced
1 large apple, grated
60 ml (2 fl oz/¼ cup) white wine
2 tablespoons apple cider vinegar

6 x 120 g (4¼ oz) pork schnitzel pieces
250 ml (9 fl oz/1 cup) buttermilk
2 garlic cloves, crushed
1 small sage sprig, finely chopped
1 teaspoon smooth, mild German mustard
seasoned plain (all-purpose) flour, for coating
3 eggs, lightly beaten
160 g (5½ oz/2 cups) breadcrumbs made from day-old bread
200 g (7 oz/2 cups) ground almonds
vegetable oil, for shallow-frying
lemon wedges, to serve

PAPRIKA CHICKEN

SERVES 6

1 tablespoon butter

2 tablespoons oil

2 small brown onions, sliced

12 chicken thighs on the bone, skin removed

1½ tablespoons Hungarian sweet paprika

1 teaspoon Hungarian hot paprika

2 garlic cloves, finely chopped

1 teaspoon soft brown sugar

2 bay leaves

160 g (5½ oz/⅔ cup) tinned chopped tomatoes

750 ml (26 fl oz/3 cups) chicken stock

250 g (9 oz/1 cup) sour cream

1 tablespoon full-cream (whole) milk

2 tablespoons flat-leaf (Italian) parsley, finely chopped

Heat half of the butter and oil in a large, deep-sided frying pan over medium–high heat. Add the onions and sauté for 5 minutes, or until lightly golden. Remove to a plate and set aside. Add the remaining butter and oil to the pan. Season the chicken with salt and freshly ground black pepper and cook, in batches, for about 4 minutes on each side, or until well browned all over. Remove the chicken to a plate.

Return the onion to the pan with the paprikas and garlic and cook for 30 seconds. Add the sugar, bay leaves, tomato and stock, stirring well to combine. Add the chicken pieces and stir. Bring to the boil, then reduce the heat and simmer for 25 minutes, or until the chicken is cooked through and tender. Remove the chicken to a bowl, cover to keep warm, and set aside. Skim the fat from the sauce and continue cooking over high heat for 15 minutes or until thickened slightly.

Put three-quarters of the sour cream in a small bowl and whisk in a spoonful of the hot liquid until smooth, then gradually stir the cream back into the sauce; allow to simmer for 2 minutes to heat through. Return the chicken to the sauce and stir to coat.

Mix the remaining sour cream with the milk and the parsley — it should be the consistency of a yoghurt sauce so it holds its shape when drizzled over the chicken.

Enjoy the chicken with the parsley sour cream drizzled over the top, if desired.

Tip: This meal is great served over hot noodles, tossed with a little butter and poppy seeds, with some lightly steamed greens on the side.

SAUERBRATEN WITH BREAD DUMPLINGS

SERVES 8

375ml (13 fl oz/1½ cups) red wine vinegar

500 ml (17 fl oz/2 cups) red wine

1½ teaspoons ground allspice

1½ teaspoons ground cinnamon

6 whole cloves

1 teaspoon black peppercorns

3 bay leaves, crumpled

1 brown onion, chopped

1 carrot, finely diced

1 celery stalk, chopped

3 garlic cloves, bruised

2 kg (4 lb 8 oz) beef topside (pot roast) rump

2 tablespoons vegetable oil

2 large brown onions, sliced, extra

1 tablespoon tomato paste (concentrated purée)

6 streaky bacon slices

60 g (2¼ oz/½ cup) raisins, plus 30 g (1 oz/¼ cup) extra, to serve

1 tablespoon butter

1½ tablespoons plain (all-purpose) flour

1 tablespoon soft brown sugar

3 gingersnap biscuits, crumbled, for serving

Put the vinegar, wine, allspice, cinnamon, cloves, peppercorns, bay leaves, onion, carrot, celery and garlic in a saucepan with 500 ml (17 fl oz/ 2 cups) water and bring to the boil. Reduce the heat and simmer for 5 minutes, then remove from the heat and cool to room temperature. Place the beef in a large non-metallic dish that will be deep enough to hold it when it is covered with the marinade. Pour the cooled marinade over the beef — it should cover it, but if it doesn't, add a little water. Cover tightly and refrigerate for 3–4 days turning a few times each day. The long marinating time gives the meat a fairly piquant flavour, if you prefer a milder result, marinate for 48 hours. Drain and reserve the marinade, then pat the beef dry with paper towels.

Heat the oil in a large flameproof casserole dish over medium–high heat and brown the meat well on all sides. Remove the meat to a plate and set aside. Add the onions to the dish and cook for about 15 minutes over medium heat, stirring occasionally, or until deep golden. Add the tomato paste and cook for 1 minute.

Meanwhile, cover the beef all over with strips of bacon, securing with toothpicks if need be. This helps prevent the meat from drying out too much during cooking. Place the beef on top of the onions, add the raisins and pour in the marinade so that it comes at least three-quarters of the way up the side of the beef. Bring to the boil, then cover with a tight-fitting lid, reduce the heat to very low and simmer for 3–3½ hours, regularly basting the top of the meat with the cooking liquid until the meat is very tender all the way through when pierced with a skewer. Make sure the liquid is always at least halfway up the meat, top up with water or a combination of half water, half wine, as needed.

Meanwhile, to make the bread dumplings, cut the bread into small cubes and place in a bowl with the breadcrumbs. Pour over the warm milk, stir to combine, then leave to rest for about 1 hour, or until the milk has been absorbed. Melt the butter in a frying pan and sauté the onion and marjoram over medium heat for 8 minutes, or until the onion is lightly golden. Add the garlic and cook for 30 seconds. Remove from the heat and allow to cool to room temperature. Use clean hands to squeeze any excess liquid from the bread, then combine well with the onion mixture, chives, egg and 1 teaspoon salt. Cover and chill until ready to cook.

Just before the beef is ready, bring a large saucepan of lightly salted water to the boil. Divide the dumpling mixture in half and form into two logs, about 5–6 cm (2–2½ inches) thick. Coat the dumplings in plain flour and carefully lower into the water, allow to come to the boil again then reduce to a simmer, cover and cook for 25 minutes, or until hot and fluffy all the way through.

When the meat is cooked, carefully lift it out of the liquid and transfer to a heatproof dish, cover, and keep warm in a low oven. To finish the sauce, strain the cooking liquid into a pitcher, discarding the solids. Melt the butter in a saucepan over medium heat, add the flour and cook for 1 minute, then gradually whisk in 2 cups of the strained cooking liquid until smooth. Add the sugar and extra raisins and stir for 5 minutes or until the sauce boils and thickens, adding any juices from the meat.

Remove the bacon from the beef and discard. Carefully slice the beef as it will be very tender and about to fall apart. Place it on a lipped platter, pour over the sauce and crumble over the gingersnap biscuits

When the dumplings are cooked, remove from the pan with a slotted spoon and drain on a clean tea towel (dish towel). Use a serrated knife to cut the dumplings into thick slices. Serve alongside the beef.

Variation: If you prefer, serve the sauerbraten with spaetzle (page 190) (simply cook in boiling water instead of the beetroot juice) or mashed potatoes instead of the bread dumplings. This dish is also good with a lamb or pork leg or shoulder, but omit the bacon with those variations.

BREAD DUMPLINGS

8 x 2 cm (¾ inch) thick slices of two-day-old sourdough bread, with crusts
160 g (5½ oz/2 cups) fresh white breadcrumbs
310 ml (10¾ fl oz/1¼ cups) warm full-cream (whole) milk
2 tablespoons butter
1 brown onion, finely chopped
½ teaspoon ground marjoram
3 garlic cloves, crushed
1 handful chives, snipped
2 eggs, lightly beaten
plain (all-purpose) flour, for coating

MUSTARD-ROASTED TURKEY WITH SPECK POTATOES AND HONEY SAUCE

SERVES 6

Preheat the oven to 180°C (350°F/Gas 4). Combine the butter, mustard, garlic, sage and lemon zest and carefully insert under the skin, over the turkey breast, ensuring the skin doesn't tear. Rub the oil over the outside of the breast, spreading the butter evenly underneath as you go. Season with salt and a little freshly ground black pepper. Place on a wire rack in a roasting tin. Pour the chicken stock into the tin. Place in the oven and cook for 1 hour 5 minutes, basting regularly with the pan juices until the skin is golden all over and the meat feels firm to the touch, only yielding slightly.

Meanwhile, bring a large saucepan of water to the boil and cook the potato for a few minutes, or until just starting to become tender. Drain well. Heat the oil and butter in another saucepan over medium heat and cook the onion and speck until very lightly golden, then combine with the potatoes. Tip into a roasting tin and place in the oven for the final 15 minutes of the turkey's cooking time.

When the turkey is cooked, remove from the oven, cover lightly with foil and set aside to rest for 10–15 minutes. Keep the potatoes in the oven during this time so they become lightly golden. When done, remove from the oven, season with salt, to taste.

While the turkey is resting, make the sauce. Combine all the ingredients in a saucepan along with any cooking juices from the turkey roasting tin and carefully bring to the boil over medium–high heat — make sure it doesn't boil over. Reduce the heat to low and simmer for 10 minutes. Tip in any resting juices from the turkey and continue to simmer until slightly glazy.

Slice the turkey and serve with the sauce and potatoes on the side. This dish tastes great with some lightly cooked green vegetables such as kale, spinach or green beans on the side.

Variation: You can also use this recipe for roasted chicken or poussin (baby chicken) — just adjust the cooking times accordingly.

4 tablespoons butter, softened
1½ tablespoons German-style grain mustard
2 garlic cloves, crushed
1½ teaspoons finely chopped sage
½ teaspoon finely grated lemon zest
1 tablespoon vegetable oil
1.6 kg (3 lb 8 oz) boneless turkey breast, skin on
375 ml (13 fl oz/1½ cups) chicken stock

1 kg (2 lb 4 oz) all-purpose potatoes, such as desiree, cut into 1.5 cm (⅝ inch) dice
2 tablespoons vegetable oil
1 tablespoon butter
1 large brown onion, finely sliced
50 g (1¾ oz) speck, finely diced

HONEY SAUCE
60 ml (2 fl oz/¼ cup) honey
2 tablespoons Bärenjäger or European honey liqueur
80 ml (2½ fl oz/⅓ cup) chicken stock
1 bay leaf
1 tablespoon butter
a dash of freshly squeezed lemon juice

PORK IN MILK WITH POLENTA CRUST

SERVES 6

3 tablespoons butter
1 brown onion, chopped
1 celery stalk, chopped
1 large carrot, cut into small dice
1 kg (2 lb 4 oz) skinless, boneless pork
   shoulder or leg meat
a pinch of white pepper
125 ml (4 fl oz/½ cup) dry white wine
1.25 litres (44 fl oz/5 cups) full-cream
   (whole) milk
1 bay leaf
1 sage sprig, finely chopped
1 small rosemary sprig, leaves finely chopped
2 strips lemon zest, white pith removed
1 tablespoon freshly squeezed lemon juice
2 garlic cloves, crushed
½ teaspoon freshly grated nutmeg
1½ tablespoons pouring (whipping) cream

POLENTA
375 ml (13 fl oz/1½ cups) chicken stock
100 g (3½ oz/⅔ cup) instant polenta
1½ tablespoons butter
1 egg, lightly beaten

Heat half of the butter in a large saucepan over medium–high heat and add the onion, celery and carrot. Cook for 8 minutes, or until the onion is lightly golden. Remove from the pan and set aside.

Meanwhile, cut the pork meat into 2 cm (¾ inch) cubes, season with salt and a little white pepper and toss to combine. Add the remaining butter to the pan and, in batches, brown the pork well. Return all the pork and vegetables to the pan with the wine, milk, herbs, lemon zest, lemon juice, garlic and nutmeg. Bring to the boil, then reduce the heat and simmer for 1½ hours, or until the pork is very tender. Remove the solids with a slotted spoon and set aside in a large bowl. Discard the bay leaf. (The sauce will have separated and look lumpy — this is normal.) Allow the sauce to cool slightly, then blend in a food processor or with a stick blender, and stir in the cream. Combine with the pork and vegetable mixture and season to taste. Divide between six 375 ml (13 fl oz/1½ cup) individual ramekins, cool slightly, then refrigerate while you make the polenta.

Preheat the oven to 180°C (350°F/Gas 4). To cook the polenta, put the stock in a saucepan with 375 ml (13 fl oz/1½ cups) water and bring to the boil. Gradually add the polenta in a fine stream, whisking constantly. Stir for 5–8 minutes, or until the polenta is thick and smooth. Remove from the heat, whisk in the butter and season to taste. While still warm and soft, carefully divide between the filled ramekins and smooth over. Cool slightly to allow the polenta to firm. Brush the tops with the egg. Cook the pies for 25–30 minutes, or until the top is crispy and the filling is heated through. Serve with cooked green vegetables, such as green beans or kale, or a bitter leaf salad.

CHICKEN FRICASSEE

SERVES 6–8

Put the chicken livers in a small bowl, cover with milk and soak overnight in the refrigerator.

Melt the butter and oil together in a large heavy-based frying pan over medium–high heat. Season the chicken cubes well with salt and freshly ground black pepper and, in batches, lightly brown all over. Set aside.

Add the leek, bacon and apples to the pan and sauté for 6 minutes, or until lightly golden. Remove from the pan and set aside. Add the Riesling and stock to the pan and use a wooden spoon to scrape up any cooked-on bits. Add the cream, herbs, blanched garlic and return the leek mixture to the pan; bring to the boil. Reduce the heat and simmer for 5 minutes, then return the chicken pieces to the pan and stir to coat in the sauce. Cover the pan and cook for 6–8 minutes, or until the chicken is cooked through and tender. Remove the chicken and vegetables from the pan and cover to keep warm. Continue cooking the sauce for a further 10–15 minutes, or until thickened.

Drain the livers and finely chop. Put them in a bowl and use a fork to mash them together with the thick cream. Stir the livers into the sauce, then mix in the mustard and cook for 30 seconds, mashing the liver so it is as smooth as possible. Season well. Return the chicken and vegetables and any resting juices to the pan and coat well in the sauce. Gently reheat. Serve the chicken fricassée with crispy golden or boiled baby potatoes or speck potatoes (see recipe, page 115) and lightly cooked greens.

150 g (5½ oz/about 3) chicken livers

250 ml (9 fl oz/1 cup) milk

2 tablespoons butter

1 tablespoon olive oil

6 boneless, skinless chicken breasts, cut into 4 cm (1½ inch) cubes

9 baby leeks, white part only, trimmed and cut in half

100 g (3½ oz) streaky bacon slices, cut into strips

2 granny smith apples, peeled, cored and each cut into 6 wedges

170 ml (5½ fl oz/⅔ cup) Riesling

375 ml (13 fl oz/1½ cups) chicken stock

250 ml (9 fl oz/1 cup) pouring (whipping) cream

2 bay leaves

1 thyme sprig, leaves finely chopped

1 small rosemary sprig, leaves finely chopped

12 garlic cloves, blanched in boiling water for 2 minutes and drained well

1 tablespoon thick (double/heavy) cream

1½ tablespoons mild German mustard

SLOW-BAKED BROWN BEANS WITH SPICE-ROASTED BACON

SERVES 6

450 g (1 lb/2½ cups) Swedish brown beans
  or pinto beans
1.25 kg (2 lb 12 oz) piece of bacon
1 large brown onion, finely chopped
2 apples, peeled, cored and finely diced
250 ml (9 fl oz/1 cup) cider vinegar
175 g (6 oz/½ cup) molasses
60 g (2¼ oz/⅓ cup) soft brown sugar
1 cinnamon stick, broken in half
2 garlic cloves, finely chopped
1½ teaspoons Hungarian sweet paprika
1 teaspoon dried marjoram
1½ teaspoons caraway seeds, lightly crushed
apple horseradish (page 131), to serve, optional

Soak the beans in plenty of water overnight.

Bring a large saucepan of water to the boil and add the whole piece of bacon. Bring back to the boil and cook for 1 hour, then remove the bacon to a plate and reserve the liquid to cook the beans.

Preheat the oven to 170°C (325°F/Gas 3). Drain the beans, then put them in the base of a large roasting tin with the onion. Pour in just enough of the reserved cooking liquid to cover the beans (about 3 cups). Cover tightly with foil and cook in the oven for 2½ hours. Remove from the oven.

Stir the apple, vinegar, molasses, sugar, cinnamon stick and garlic into the beans. Place a roasting rack over the top, making sure the rack is high enough to not be touching the beans.

Carefully remove the rind from the bacon so that the fat layer is exposed. Combine the paprika, marjoram and caraway and sprinkle over the top of the bacon. Place the bacon, fat side up, on top of the rack and return to the oven. Cook for 45 minutes, or until the bacon is very tender. If the beans are not thick and saucy by this stage, remove the bacon and keep warm. Increase the oven temperature to 200°C (400°F/Gas 6) and keep cooking for 5–10 minutes, or until rich and thick.

Thickly slice the bacon and serve over the beans with the apple horseradish, if desired. It also goes well with boiled or mashed potatoes and lightly cooked greens on the side.

NORDIC SEAFOOD HOTPOT

SERVES 6

Use clean tweezers to remove any visible bones from the cod and salmon and cut the fillets into 3 cm (1¼ in) square pieces. Cover with plastic wrap and refrigerate until ready to use.

Heat the oil and butter in a large saucepan or stockpot over medium heat. Add the onion, celery, carrot and bay leaf and cook for 10 minutes, stirring occasionally, until lightly golden.

Add the tomato paste and garlic and cook for 1 minute. Add the vodka, stock, 750 ml (26 fl oz/3 cups) water, herring, thyme, chillies, saffron, coriander, juniper berries and orange. Bring to the boil, then reduce the heat and simmer for 30 minutes. Add the potatoes and cook for about 8 minutes, or until the potatoes are just tender.

Add the fish pieces and prawns and continue simmering for 2–3 minutes, or until the prawns start to curl. Add the oysters and cook for 1 minute further. Remove from the heat and stir through the orange juice; season to taste.

Serve the seafood in wide shallow bowls with a fork and a spoon so you can eat the broth. Serve with Scandinavian-style crispbreads smeared with good butter, or fresh bread to mop up the juices.

600 g (1 lb 5 oz) cod fillets or other firm white fish fillets
300 g (10½ oz) salmon fillets
1 tablespoon vegetable oil
2 tablespoons butter
1 large brown onion, finely chopped
1 celery stalk, finely diced
2 carrots, finely diced
1 bay leaf
2½ tablespoons tomato paste (concentrated purée)
1 garlic clove, crushed
170 ml (5½ fl oz/⅔ cup) vodka
1 litre (35 fl oz/4 cups) mild fish stock
1 herring, rinsed and very finely chopped
1 thyme sprig, leaves finely chopped
3 small red chillies
a large pinch of saffron threads
1 teaspoon ground coriander
1 teaspoon juniper berries
2 long strips orange zest, white pith removed
18 baby potatoes, peeled
18 raw king prawns (shrimp), peeled and deveined, tails left intact
12 oysters, removed from the shell
1 tablespoon freshly squeezed orange juice, strained

PAPRIKA PORK CUTLETS WITH RED PEPPER SAUCE AND NOODLE KUGEL

SERVES 4

2 large red capsicums (peppers)
4 tablespoons olive oil
1 brown onion, finely chopped
1 teaspoon caraway seeds
2 teaspoons Hungarian sweet paprika
2 garlic cloves
1 bay leaf
2½ tablespoons apple cider vinegar
2 teaspoons soft brown sugar
½ teaspoon Hungarian hot paprika
1 teaspoon sea salt
4 x 200 g (7 oz) pork cutlets

KUGEL
200 g (7 oz/2 cups) cooked short egg noodles
   (see note)
185 g (6½ oz/¾ cup) sour cream
60 ml (2 fl oz/¼ cup) chicken stock
2 large eggs
1 brown onion, grated and squeezed to
   extract moisture
a large handful of flat-leaf (Italian) parsley,
   finely chopped

Preheat the oven to 200°C (400°F/Gas 6). Roast the whole capsicums for 20–25 minutes or until blistered and starting to blacken. Remove from the heat, place in a bowl and cover with plastic wrap until cool enough to handle. Peel the capsicum, discarding the skin, inner membrane and seeds, and purée in a food processor until smooth. Set aside.

Meanwhile, heat half the oil in a saucepan over medium heat. Add the onion and caraway seeds and cook for 10 minutes, or until the onion is golden. Add the sweet paprika, garlic and bay leaf and stir well, then add the vinegar and the sugar and bring to the boil.

Stir the capsicum purée into the pan and bring to the boil over high heat. Reduce the heat and simmer for 5 minutes, or until thickened. Season to taste and set aside until ready to serve, reheating gently if necessary.

Reduce the oven temperature to 170°C (325°F/Gas 3). To make the kugel, combine all the ingredients in a bowl, season well, then pour into four 250 ml (9 fl oz/1 cup) well-buttered ramekins or a 1 litre (35 fl oz/4 cup) shallow baking dish. Cook in the oven for 8 minutes for individual ramekins or 12–15 minutes for large baking dish — the kugel should be just set and lightly golden on top.

While the kugel is cooking, combine the hot paprika with the sea salt and a little pepper. Rub all over the pork cutlets. Heat the remaining oil in a large heavy-based frying pan over medium–high heat and cook the cutlets for 4 minutes on each side, or until just cooked through. Remove from the heat and rest for 5 minutes before serving. Stir any resting juices into the sauce. Serve the pork cutlets with the red pepper sauce and an individual kugel, or a wedge of the larger kugel.

Variation: You can also use lamb cutlets for this recipe — allow 3–5 for each person depending on appetite.

Note: If you can't find short egg noodles, just break vermicelli or spaghettini into short lengths.

OSSO BUCCO WITH SAFFRON RISOTTO

SERVES 4–6

4 tablespoons olive oil

1 tablespoon butter

1 large brown onion, finely chopped

1 large carrot, finely diced

1 large celery stalk, finely diced

1 bay leaf

12 x 3 cm (1¼ inch) thick pieces of veal shank (veal osso bucco), about 1.8–2 kg (4–4 lb 8 oz)

seasoned plain (all-purpose) flour, for coating

250 ml (9 fl oz/1 cup) white wine

60 ml (2 fl oz/¼ cup) freshly squeezed lemon juice

1 large strip lemon rind, white pith removed

500 ml (17 fl oz/2 cups) veal or chicken stock

1 large thyme sprig, leaves finely chopped

¼ teaspoon finely grated nutmeg

Heat half of the oil and half of the butter over medium heat in a deep, flameproof casserole dish with a lid. Add the onion, carrot, celery and bay leaf and cook, for 15–20 minutes, stirring often, until lightly golden. Remove the vegetables from the dish and set aside.

Lightly coat the veal pieces in the seasoned flour. Add a little more oil and the remaining butter to the dish. Working in batches, brown the veal pieces well on each side, adding a little more oil if needed. Remove from the dish and set aside.

Add the wine, lemon juice and zest, stock, thyme and nutmeg to the dish, scraping up any cooked-on bits with a wooden spoon. Return the veal pieces to the dish along with the vegetables and stir well to combine. Bring to the boil, then reduce the heat, cover, and simmer for 1½ hours. Remove the lid and cook for a further 30–45 minutes, or until the veal is very tender but not quite falling off the bone. Discard the lemon zest. Carefully remove the meat from the dish, cover, and keep warm. Increase the heat and cook the sauce for a further 15 minutes, or until thickened. Return the meat to the dish and carefully turn to coat in the sauce. Season to taste.

Meanwhile, to make the risotto, combine the saffron threads with the wine and set aside. Put the stock and 375 ml (13 fl oz/1½ cups) water in a saucepan and bring to the boil, then immediately reduce to a simmer.

Melt half the butter in a large saucepan over medium heat and sauté the onion for 5 minutes, or until softened. Add the rice and cook for 2 minutes, stirring constantly, until the rice becomes translucent. Add the saffron and wine to the simmering stock. Ladle in ½ cup of the simmering stock into the rice and stir constantly until all the liquid has been absorbed. Continue to stir in the stock, ½ cup at a time, ensuring the liquid is absorbed before adding more, until all the stock has been used and the rice is tender and creamy — this will take about 25 minutes. Remove from the heat and stir through the remaining butter and parmesan. Season to taste.

Combine all the gremolata ingredients and chop again to combine the flavours.

Spoon some risotto into wide shallow bowls or plates and top with the osso bucco. Sprinkle with the gremolata and serve immediately.

Tip: Serve some lightly cooked baby peas or other greens as a side.

Note: Any leftover risotto can be formed into small balls when cold, crumbed and deep-fried as a warm snack.

SAFFRON RISOTTO

a large pinch of saffron threads
125 ml (4 fl oz/½ cup) white wine
1.25 litre (44 fl oz/5 cups) chicken stock
125 g (4½ oz) butter
1 large brown onion, finely chopped
330 g (11½ oz/1½ cups) risotto rice
50 g (1¾ oz/½ cup) finely grated parmesan cheese

GREMOLATA

2 garlic cloves, very finely chopped
2 teaspoons finely grated lemon zest
2 large handfuls flat-leaf (Italian) parsley, finely chopped

GARLICKY PELMENI WITH BROWN BUTTER, HERBS AND YOGHURT

SERVES 4–6

DOUGH
300 g (10½ oz/2 cups) plain (all-purpose) flour
2 eggs

PELMENI FILLING
1 tablespoon butter
1 small brown onion, finely chopped
150 g (5½ oz) minced (ground) veal
250 g (9 oz) minced (ground) pork
80 g (2¾ oz/1 cup) fresh white breadcrumbs
3 garlic cloves, very finely chopped
¼ teaspoon white pepper
¼ teaspoon freshly grated nutmeg
60 g (2¼ oz/¼ cup) sour cream

Begin by making the dough — combine the flour and 1 teaspoon salt in a bowl and make a well in the centre. Lightly beat the eggs and 60 ml (2 fl oz/¼ cup) water together, then pour into the well. Use your hands to mix the flour into the liquid until the mixture comes together and you can gather it into a ball — the dough will be fairly stiff. Turn out onto a lightly floured work surface and knead for about 10 minutes, or until smooth and elastic. Wrap in plastic wrap and refrigerate for 2 hours.

Meanwhile, to make the filling, melt the butter in a frying pan over medium heat. Add the onion and cook for about 8 minutes, stirring occasionally until lightly golden. Remove from the heat and cool slightly. Season with salt. Mix together with the meats, breadcrumbs, garlic, white pepper, nutmeg and sour cream until thoroughly combined. Season to taste and knead in the bowl for a few minutes. Cover and refrigerate until the dough is ready.

Remove the dough from the fridge and divide into two pieces. Roll out the first piece of dough until it's about 2 mm (1/16 inch) thick. Using a 4 cm (1½ inch) cutter, cut 16 rounds from the dough. Roll each round out to 5–6 cm (2–2½ inches) in diameter. Repeat with the remaining dough.

Place 2 teaspoons of the filling in the centre of each round. Dip a finger into water and run around the edge of half the dough. Fold the opposite side over to meet the dampened side, then seal the edges by pressing together with your fingers. Bring the two corners up to meet in the centre of the rounded, sealed side of the dough and pinch together tightly to form a triangular pouch similar to a tortellini. Refrigerate until ready to cook.

When ready to cook, put the stock, bay leaves, lemon zest and a dash of lemon juice into a large saucepan and bring to the boil. Add half the pelmeni and cook for 5 minutes, stirring occasionally so they don't stick together, until the pelmeni rise to the surface. Lift out into a bowl with a little of the broth. Cover to keep warm.

Add the remaining pelmeni to the stock and just before they finish cooking, add the first half of the pelmeni and any liquid back to the pan to heat through. Remove the pelmeni with a large slotted spoon and divide between four wide bowls. Sprinkle over the radish, chives and dill.

Just before the pelmeni has finished cooking, heat the butter in a saucepan over medium heat until just melted, then reduce the heat and swirl the pan occasionally until the butter just starts to take on a golden colour and nutty aroma — about 3–5 minutes (watch it carefully as it can go from browned to burnt very quickly). Add a splash of the extra lemon juice and immediately drizzle over the top of the pelmeni, then dollop each serving with a little yoghurt. Sprinkle with the grated nutmeg and serve straight away.

While diners are enjoying the pelmeni, remove the bay leaves and lemon zest from the simmering stock, add the greens and cook for a few minutes or until tender. Stir in the remaining lemon juice, season to taste, and serve as a refreshing broth after the rich pelmeni.

Tip: If you don't have time to make the pelmeni dough, you can use round won ton wrappers instead. The whole recipe can also easily be doubled to serve 8–12, or half of the pelmeni can be frozen for later use — it will last up to 3 months stored in an airtight container in the freezer.

Variations: Instead of the brown butter and yoghurt, you can simply serve the pelmeni in the broth with the greens, as a dumpling soup. Pelmeni can also be filled with a variety of other ingredients: chicken or fish mince; mushrooms; spring onions (scallions); or cabbage. Choose an appropriate stock to cook them in, or try them deep-fried.

2.5 litres (88 fl oz/10 cups) veal or chicken stock
2 bay leaves
2 strips of lemon zest, white pith removed
a dash of freshly squeezed lemon juice, plus 1½ tablespoons extra
4 radishes, very finely julienned
1 small handful chives, snipped
1 large handful dill, chopped
180 g (6¼ oz) butter
90 g (3¼ oz/⅓ cup) Greek-style yoghurt, to serve
freshly grated nutmeg, to garnish
300 g (10½ oz) finely shredded spinach leaves, bitter greens or cabbage

CRISP ROAST PORK HOCK WITH SPICED RED CABBAGE AND APPLE HORSERADISH

SERVES 4

Preheat the oven to 220°C (425°F/Gas 7). Place a large wire rack in a roasting tin. Stand the hocks upright on the rack, balancing them against each other with the small end pointing up. Rub well with sea salt. Cook for 1 hour, then reduce the temperature to 160°C (315°F/ Gas 2–3). Pour a small amount of water under the rack and cook for 1 hour further. Increase the temperature back to 220°C (425°F/Gas 7) and cook for a further 30 minutes, or until the pork is very tender, dark golden and crispy. Remove from the oven, cover, and rest for about 10 minutes before serving.

While the hocks are cooking, make the spiced red cabbage. Melt the butter in a large saucepan over medium–high heat. Add the onion and cabbage and stir for 10 minutes, or until the cabbage has wilted slightly. Add the rest of the ingredients, except the allspice, and stir to combine. Cover, reduce the heat and simmer for 40 minutes, stirring occasionally, until the cabbage is tender and there is very little liquid left. Stir in the allspice and season to taste. Turn off the heat and cover to keep warm.

For the apple horseradish, combine the apple sauce and horseradish and mix well. Set aside.

Serve the hocks on top of some cabbage with the apple horseradish sauce on the side.

Tip: This dish is perfect with smooth mashed potatoes whipped together with a good dollop of mild, savoury mustard and some tender steamed green beans or spinach.

4 x 750 g (1 lb 10 oz) fresh pork hocks from the hind legs, lightly scored around the hock
2 tablespoons sea salt

SPICED RED CABBAGE
60 g (2¼ oz) butter
1 red onion, finely sliced
1.5 kg (3 lb 5 oz/about ½ large head) red cabbage, thickly shredded
65 g (2½ oz/½ cup) dried cranberries
1 granny smith apple, peeled, cored and grated
6 juniper berries
60 ml (2 fl oz/¼ cup) red wine
3 tablespoons red wine vinegar
1 bay leaf
½ teaspoon freshly grated nutmeg
3 tablespoons soft brown sugar
½ teaspoon ground allspice

APPLE HORSERADISH
65 g (2½ oz/¼ cup) apple sauce
2 tablespoons bottled horseradish

KURNIK CHICKEN PIE

SERVES 8

PASTRY

425 g (15 oz/2¾ cups) plain (all-purpose) flour
¼ teaspoon baking powder
1 tablespoon caster (superfine) sugar
150 g (5½ oz) butter, melted and cooled slightly
125 g (4½ oz/½ cup) crème fraîche or Smetana
  (see note), plus 2 tablespoons, extra
1 egg

To make the pastry, sift the flour, baking powder, sugar and 1 teaspoon salt into a bowl. Make a well in the centre. Combine the melted butter and crème fraîche and pour into the well. Mix with a flat-bladed knife until the mixture comes together in clumps, then turn out onto a lightly floured surface and knead lightly for a few minutes until smooth. Roll into a ball, flatten slightly into a disc, then cover in plastic wrap and refrigerate for 1 hour. Remove from the fridge 10 minutes before rolling.

To make the filling, place the chicken in a large saucepan or stockpot and cover with 3 litres (105 fl oz/12 cups) cold water. Add the cloves, peppercorns, celery and bay leaves. Bring to the boil over high heat, then simmer for 1 hour, or until the chicken is cooked through. Skim off any foam that rises to the surface. Remove the chicken from the pan and set aside. Leave the pan on the heat and bring the stock back to the boil. Cook for 30–35 minutes, or until reduced by half, then strain and reserve. Meanwhile, when the chicken is cool enough to handle, remove and discard the skin, then pull the meat from the bones. Cut into bite-sized pieces. Refrigerate until ready to use.

Put one-quarter of the butter in a large frying pan over medium–high heat and add the mushrooms. Sauté for 4–5 minutes, or until softened, and set aside. Add half of the remaining butter and the onion to the pan and cook, stirring regularly for 15 minutes or until lightly golden. Add the nutmeg and garlic and stir for 30 seconds before returning the mushrooms to the pan. Season with salt and a little white pepper and combine well.

Bring the strained stock to the boil again and add the rice. Cook for 10 minutes, or until very tender but not mushy. Strain again, reserving the stock. Mix the rice into the mushroom mixture with the lemon juice. Set aside.

Melt the remaining butter over medium high heat in a saucepan and add the flour. Stir for 1 minute. Gradually whisk in 2 cups of the reserved stock. Slowly bring to the boil and cook for 3–5 minutes, stirring regularly until thickened and smooth. Whisk a little of the sauce into the crème fraîche to thin, then tip this mixture back into the saucepan with the eggs, herbs and reserved chicken. Combine well and season, to taste.

Preheat the oven to 190°C (375°F/Gas 5). Grease a 3 litre (105 fl oz/12 cup) baking dish, about 5 cm (2 inches) deep, with the extra butter. Spread half the rice mixture over the base, then top with half the chicken. Repeat with the remaining rice and chicken and smooth over the top.

Roll the pastry out on a lightly floured sheet of baking paper until it is just a little larger than the baking dish. Invert the pastry over the dish and peel off the paper. Trim the edges, then make decorations with the pastry scraps. As this pie is traditionally made for festive occasions, particularly Russian weddings, simple flowers are appropriate, but you can decorate however you like — or not at all!

Combine the egg with the extra crème fraîche and whisk to combine. Brush liberally over the top of the pie. Bake in the oven for 40–45 minutes, or until the top is golden and the filling is heated through. Serve with vegetables or salad.

Note: Smetana is similar to crème fraîche, but much heavier and native to Central and Eastern Europe.

FILLING

1.8 kg (4 lb) whole chicken
3 whole cloves
1 teaspoon black peppercorns
2 celery stalks, finely chopped
2 bay leaves
100 g (3½ oz) butter, plus extra for greasing
300 g (10½ oz) fresh porcini (cep) mushrooms or cap mushrooms, sliced
3 large brown onions, sliced
¾ teaspoon freshly grated nutmeg
3 garlic cloves, very finely chopped
white pepper, for seasoning
135 g (4¾ oz/⅔ cup) white medium-grain rice
1 teaspoon freshly squeezed lemon juice
2½ tablespoons plain (all-purpose) flour
375 g (13 oz/1½ cups) crème fraîche or Smetana (see note)
5 large hard-boiled eggs, peeled and finely chopped
2 large handfuls dill, chopped
1 large handful flat-leaf (Italian) parsley, chopped
1 handful chives, snipped

RABBIT IN RED WINE WITH SPINACH CANEDERLI

SERVES 4

1.6 kg (3 lb 8 oz/1 whole) farmed white rabbit, kidney and liver removed and discarded, cut into 8 pieces

3 red onions, cut into wedges

2 carrots, thickly sliced on an angle

2 celery stalks, diced

75 g (2½ oz) pancetta, diced

80 ml (2½ fl oz/⅓ cup) olive oil

310 ml (10¼ fl oz/1¼ cups) red wine

185 ml (6 fl oz/¾ cup) Marsala

2 garlic cloves, crushed

1½ teaspoons ground cinnamon

½ teaspoon freshly ground nutmeg

a pinch of ground cloves

1½ teaspoons juniper berries

2 bay leaves

2 teaspoons finely chopped sage

Preheat the oven to 240°C (475°F/Gas 8). Put the rabbit pieces, onion wedges, carrot, celery and pancetta in a roasting tin. Drizzle over the oil, season with a little salt and freshly ground black pepper and toss well to coat. Place in the oven and cook for 10 minutes, or until the rabbit and vegetables are lightly golden. Remove from the oven and reduce the heat to 160°C (315°F/Gas 2–3). Add the wine, Marsala, 500 ml (17 fl oz/2 cups) water, garlic, cinnamon, nutmeg, cloves, juniper berries, bay leaves and sage to the tin and stir gently to combine. Cover tightly with foil and cook for 2½ hours, or until the rabbit is very tender. The rabbit should be covered at all times.

While the rabbit is cooking, make the canederli. Dice the bread, put in a shallow dish and pour over the milk — set aside for about 20 minutes or until most of the milk has been absorbed. Meanwhile, put the spinach leaves in a bowl and pour over enough boiling water to make the spinach completely wilt. Drain well and when cool, squeeze the spinach dry in a clean tea towel (dish towel). Very finely chop the spinach and set aside.

Squeeze the bread to extract the excess milk and discard the milk. Put the bread and the spinach in the bowl of a food processor with a large pinch of salt, the nutmeg and a little freshly ground black pepper. Process until smooth, then tip into a bowl and stir in the egg, combining well. Gradually stir in the flour, one tablespoon at a time, until the mixture forms a soft, pliable dough — it should not be sloppy. Sprinkle with a little extra flour and knead briefly just to bring the mixture together.

Roll the mixture into a 2 cm (¾ inch) thick rope on the bench, using flat hands, then slice into 3 cm (1¼ inch) lengths. Set aside until ready to cook.

When the rabbit is cooked remove it from the liquid, place in a bowl and cover to keep warm. Heat two burners on your stove to high and place the roasting tin on top. Cook for 25 minutes, stirring occasionally, until the sauce has thickened slightly — you may need to hold the tin still with an oven-mitted hand. Return the rabbit pieces to the tin and carefully turn to coat in the sauce. Remove from the heat and cover with foil to keep warm.

While the sauce is reducing, bring a large saucepan of salted water to the boil. Add the canederli and cook for 5 minutes, or until they float to the surface. Drain in a colander.

Melt the butter and oil in a large non-stick frying pan over high heat. Add the canederli and cook, in batches, for 5 minutes each, or until lightly golden and slightly crisp, shaking the pan occasionally.

Serve two pieces of rabbit per person, with the sauce spooned over and the canederli on the side. Garnish with the sage.

Tip: Canederli is a great accompaniment to other stews and casseroles, or used in place of gnocchi with your favourite sauce.

SPINACH CANEDERLI

300 g (10½ oz) day-old crusty bread, crusts removed
250 ml (9 fl oz/1 cup) full-cream (whole) milk
350 g (12 oz) English spinach leaves, rinsed and drained
¼ teaspoon freshly grated nutmeg
1 egg, lightly beaten
50 g (1¾ oz/⅓ cup) plain (all-purpose) flour, sifted
1 tablespoon butter
1 tablespoon extra virgin olive oil

MEATBALLS WITH VODKA DILL CREAM SAUCE

SERVES 4–6

Combine the breadcrumbs and 125 ml (4 fl oz/½ cup) of the cream and leave to sit until the breadcrumbs have soaked up all the liquid. Add the beef and pork mince, egg, onion, nutmeg, allspice, salt and white pepper and combine well. Roll the mixture into 3 cm (1¼ inch) balls and place in a single layer on a baking tray lined with baking paper. Cover and refrigerate for 3–4 hours to allow the flavours to develop.

When ready to cook, heat half of the butter with the oil in a large heavy-based frying pan over a medium–high heat (do not use a non-stick pan). Cook the meatballs, in batches, for 4–6 minutes each, or until browned all over. Remove and set aside.

Add the remaining butter and the flour to the pan and stir. Gradually whisk in the hot stock and remaining cream, scraping up any cooked-on bits. Add the dill and 3 tablespoons of the vodka, and bring to the boil, whisking continuously until smooth and thickened slightly. Return the meatballs to the pan, along with any resting juices, and cook for 10 minutes or until tender. Stir through the remaining vodka and season to taste. Garnish with the fresh dill and serve with lingonberry preserves as a condiment.

Tip: Serve the meatballs over some sautéed or mashed potatoes, or buttered noodles, with the lingonberry preserves on the side as a condiment. A shot of vodka is a must!

160 g (5½ oz/2 cups) fresh white breadcrumbs
185 ml (6 fl oz/¾ cup) pouring (whipping) cream
350 g (12 oz) minced (ground) beef
350 g (12 oz) minced (ground) pork
1 large egg
1 brown onion, very finely chopped
¼ teaspoon freshly grated nutmeg
a pinch of ground allspice
1 teaspoon fine sea salt
¼ teaspoon white pepper
2 tablespoons butter
1 tablespoon oil
1 tablespoon plain (all-purpose) flour
435 ml (15¼ fl oz/1¾ cups) hot beef stock
1½ tablespoons chopped dill, plus extra to garnish
80 ml (2½ fl oz/⅓ cup) vodka
lingonberry preserves, to serve

CABBAGE ROLLS

MAKES 12 / SERVES 6

120 g (4¼ oz/1½ cups) fresh white
  breadcrumbs
170 ml (5½ fl oz/⅔ cup) full-cream (whole) milk
350 g (12 oz) minced (ground) pork
200 g (7 oz) minced (ground) turkey or chicken
1 brown onion, grated and squeezed to extract
  excess moisture
1 small celery sick, very finely diced
½ small green capsicum (pepper), very
  finely diced
1 teaspoon finely chopped marjoram
1 small handful chives, finely snipped
½ teaspoon celery salt
1½ teaspoons Hungarian sweet paprika, plus
  extra to serve
3 garlic cloves, very finely chopped
1 egg, beaten
1 whole green cabbage
1 litre (35 fl oz/4 cups) chicken stock
125 ml (4 fl oz/½ cup) cider vinegar
3 bay leaves
2 teaspoons black peppercorns
3 whole cloves
melted butter, optional, to serve
plain yoghurt, optional, to serve

Put the breadcrumbs in a bowl and cover with the milk. Stir to combine and set aside.

Put the pork and turkey mince into a bowl with the onion, celery, capsicum, marjoram, chives, celery salt, paprika, garlic and the egg. Use very clean hands to mix together until well combined. Add the breadcrumb and milk mixture and mix again with your hands until well combined. Cover with plastic wrap and refrigerate for 2 hours.

Bring a large saucepan of water to the boil. Remove the core of the cabbage with a small sharp knife, and then add the cabbage to the boiling water, core side down. When the leaves start to loosen, use tongs to pull them away from the cabbage head and allow them to wilt completely before removing and draining in a large colander. Continue peeling off leaves as they loosen. Set aside the twelve largest leaves for the rolls. Finely chop two extra leaves. Set the rest aside for lining the pan; reserve the cabbage water.

Add the finely chopped cabbage leaves to the filling mixture, season with salt and freshly ground black pepper and combine well. Divide the filling mixture into 12 even portions, approximately one-third of a cup each, and roll each into a short, fat log shape.

When cool enough to handle, place one of the 12 large cabbage leaves onto your work surface, vein side down, with the rounded edge facing away from you. Cut out a small upside down 'V' shape from the edge closest to you.

Place one log of the mixture horizontally, just above the 'V' and roll up the cabbage leaves, folding in the sides like you would for a spring roll. Repeat with the remaining filling and leaves.

Line the base of a deep heavy-based saucepan or stockpot with two-thirds of the leftover cabbage leaves and then place the cabbage rolls, seam side down, on top of them in a single layer — it should be a snug fit. Pour 1 litre (35 fl oz/4 cups) of the reserved cabbage water over the top and add the chicken stock, vinegar, bay leaves, peppercorns and cloves to the pan. Cover with the remaining cabbage leaves and place over high heat. Bring to the boil, then reduce the heat, cover with a lid, and simmer for 45 minutes, or until cooked through. Test one of the rolls by cutting in half — they are ready when the filling is completely cooked through.

Lift out as many cabbage rolls as needed with a slotted spoon or tongs. Any leftovers can be stored in the refrigerator for up to 4 days in the liquid they were cooked in, and can be reheated gently in the same liquid. Serve immediately with melted butter or yoghurt for drizzling over, and paprika to dust.

Tip: Cabbage rolls can be enjoyed as a hearty snack or as a main meal with vegetables on the side.

LASAGNE VERDE

SERVES 6–8

VEAL FILLING

3 tablespoons butter

1 tablespoon olive oil

1 brown onion, finely chopped

50 g (1¾ oz) prosciutto, finely chopped

3 garlic cloves, finely chopped

1 kg (2 lb 4 oz) minced (ground) veal

75 g (2½ oz) chicken livers, trimmed and
   very finely chopped

1 teaspoon dried porcini (cep) mushrooms,
   crumbled

1 teaspoon freshly grated nutmeg

1 teaspoon finely chopped sage

½ teaspoon very finely chopped rosemary

1 bay leaf

60 ml (2 fl oz/¼ cup) white wine

500 ml (17 fl oz/2 cups) chicken stock

875 ml (30 fl oz/3½ cups) full-cream
   (whole) milk

3 tablespoons plain (all-purpose) flour

To make the veal filling, heat 1 tablespoon of the butter with the oil in a large saucepan over medium–high heat. Add the onion and prosciutto and sauté for 10 minutes, or until lightly golden. Add the garlic and cook for 30 seconds and then add the veal mince, stirring it with a spoon to break up any large lumps, until the veal just changes colour. Add the chicken livers and stir until they just change colour. Add the crumbled porcini, nutmeg, sage, rosemary and the bay leaf and stir to combine. Add the wine, stock and 375 ml (13 fl oz/1½ cups) of the milk, and just bring to the boil. Immediately reduce to a simmer and cook for 2 hours 15 minutes, or until the veal is very tender.

Meanwhile gently warm the remaining milk in a small saucepan. In a separate saucepan, melt the remaining 2 tablespoons of butter over medium–high heat and then add the flour, stirring for 2 minutes. Gradually whisk in the warmed milk until you have a smooth sauce. Allow the sauce to just come to the boil, then reduce the heat and simmer for 3–4 minutes, stirring constantly, until very thick. Cover and set aside until the veal mixture is ready, then combine well. Season to taste with salt and a little freshly ground black pepper.

Preheat the oven to 190°C (375°F/Gas 5). To make the spinach filling, melt the butter in a frying pan over medium–high heat. Cook the leek for 10 minutes, or until softened. Add the spinach and nutmeg and stir for a couple of minutes, or until the spinach is wilted. Set aside.

Lightly grease a 26 x 30 x 7 cm (10½ x 12 x 2¾ inch) baking dish. Sprinkle a little of the stock over the base. Place a layer of the lasagne sheets over the base, trimming to fit. Spoon over one-third of the veal filling. Add another layer of lasagne and sprinkle lightly with a little stock, then add half of the spinach mixture, spreading it out evenly. Combine the cheeses and sprinkle one-third over the top of the spinach. Add another layer of lasagne and another one-third of the veal, followed by a layer of pasta sprinkled with a little of the stock. Spoon over the remaining spinach mixture. Sprinkle over half of the remaining cheeses. Add another layer of lasagne sheets and the remaining veal filling. Top with a final layer of lasagne and sprinkle over the remaining cheese. Combine the cream and truffle oil, if using, and drizzle over the top.

Bake in the oven for 45 minutes, or until the pasta is cooked through and tender and the top is bubbling and golden. This lasagne is very rich, so it's best when served with a crisp green salad, dressed with a sharp vinaigrette.

SPINACH FILLING
2 tablespoons butter
2 leeks, white part only, finely sliced
500 g (1 lb 2 oz) English spinach leaves, rinsed and roughly chopped
a large pinch of freshly grated nutmeg

80 ml (2½ fl oz/⅓ cup) chicken stock
500 g (1 lb 2 oz) fresh spinach lasagne sheets
300 g (10½ oz) taleggio cheese, chopped
200 g (7 oz/2 cups) grated parmesan cheese
375 ml (13 fl oz/1½ cups) pouring (whipping) cream
1 teaspoon truffle oil (optional)

SLOW-COOKED LAMB SHANKS WITH JANSSEN'S TEMPTATION

SERVES 6

1 tablespoon butter
1 tablespoon oil
6 x 300 g (10½ oz) lamb shanks
1 brown onion, finely chopped
2 garlic cloves, very finely chopped
3 anchovy fillets, finely chopped
2 teaspoons whole black peppercorns
60 ml (2 fl oz/¼ cup) brandy
60 ml (2 fl oz /¼ cup) cider vinegar
500 ml (17 fl oz/2 cups) beef stock
2½ tablespoons molasses
1 teaspoon ground allspice
1 bay leaf

JANSSEN'S TEMPTATION
4 large all-purpose potatoes, such as desiree
3 tablespoons butter
2 brown onions, finely sliced
8 anchovy fillets, very finely chopped
½ teaspoon finely chopped thyme leaves
a large pinch of white pepper
250 ml (9 fl oz/1 cup) pouring (whipping) cream
125 ml (4 fl oz/½ cup) full-cream (whole) milk
20 g (¾ oz/¼ cup) fresh white breadcrumbs

Heat the butter and oil in a large flameproof casserole dish over high heat. Season the lamb shanks and cook, in batches, until brown all over. Remove the shanks to a plate. Reduce the heat to medium, add the onion to the dish and cook for 10 minutes, or until lightly golden. Add the garlic, anchovies and peppercorns and cook for 1 minute. Carefully stir in the brandy and vinegar, scraping up any cooked-on bits. Add the stock, molasses, allspice, bay leaf and 375 ml (13 fl oz/ 1½ cups) water, stirring to combine. Return the lamb shanks to the dish, making sure the meaty part is submerged in the liquid. Bring to the boil, then reduce the heat and simmer for 2 hours, or until the meat is very tender but not falling off the bone.

Meanwhile, to make the Janssen's temptation, preheat the oven to 200°C (400°F/Gas 6). Thinly slice the potatoes using a mandolin or a very sharp knife, then cut into matchsticks. Put in a bowl and cover with water until ready to use.

Melt the butter in a frying pan over medium heat, add the onions and sauté for 10 minutes, or until softened but not coloured. Add the anchovies, thyme and white pepper and mix well. Drain the potatoes you've set aside, shaking off any excess water. Place them in a large bowl and add the onion and anchovy mixture. Season well. Using very clean hands, combine gently so you don't break up the potato matchsticks. Tip into a 30 x 25 cm (12 x 10 inch) greased baking dish. Spread out evenly.

Put the cream and milk in a saucepan and bring to a simmer over medium heat. When warm, pour over the potato mixture and press it all down so that the top is as level as possible. Sprinkle the breadcrumbs evenly over the top and cook in the oven for about 1 hour, or until the potato is tender. If the crumbs start to brown too much, cover with foil.

When the lamb shanks are cooked, transfer them to a large bowl with a slotted spoon, and cover to keep warm. Increase the heat and bring the sauce to the boil. Cook for 35–40 minutes, or until the sauce is slightly glazy. Return the shanks to the dish and carefully turn to coat.

Serve the lamb shanks with the Janssen's temptation and some lightly cooked greens.

CORIANDER ROAST CHICKEN WITH WALNUT SAUCE

SERVES 4–6

Preheat the oven to 200°C (400°F/Gas 6).

Rinse the chicken inside and out and pat dry with paper towels. Combine the softened butter with the garlic and the fresh and ground coriander. Loosen the skin over the breast by easing your fingers underneath, being careful not to tear the skin. Insert the butter between the loosened breast skin and the meat and spread around all over. Season the outside of the skin with salt and a little freshly ground black pepper. Place on a wire rack in a roasting tin. Pour 250 ml (9 fl oz/ 1 cup) water into the base. Cook for 1 hour 15 minutes, or until the juices run clear from the thickest part of the thigh after inserting a skewer. Remove from the oven, transfer the chicken to a warm plate and cover with foil to keep warm. Drain the liquid from the pan and reserve.

To make the sauce, place the roasting tin on the stovetop over two burners on medium heat. Add the butter and when it starts to sizzle add the onion and sauté for 10 minutes, or until lightly golden. Add the garlic and cook for 1 minute. Sprinkle over the flour, spices and ¼ teaspoon of freshly ground black pepper and stir quickly to combine. Add the bay leaf and gradually whisk in the reserved pan juices and enough of the stock to create a smooth thin sauce. Stir in the vinegar, walnuts and sugar, and cook for a further 2 minutes. Remove from the heat. Combine 3 tablespoons of the sauce from the roasting tin with the egg yolks, quickly mixing until smooth. Stir this egg mixture back into the tin and whisk to combine well.

Place back on the two burners, now over a low heat, and whisk constantly for 2 minutes, or until the mixture thickens again slightly. Be careful not to let it boil. Remove from the heat and season to taste. Carve the chicken and serve with the walnut sauce on the side for spooning over.

Tip: Serve with some lightly cooked vegetables, such as new potatoes, baby carrots or cabbage tossed with a little butter and chopped fresh coriander.

2 kg (4 lb 8 oz) whole chicken
80 g (2¾ oz) butter, softened
1 garlic clove, very finely chopped
a large handful of coriander (cilantro) leaves, finely chopped
¼ teaspoon ground coriander

WALNUT SAUCE

1 tablespooon butter
1 small brown onion, very finely chopped
5 garlic cloves, crushed
2 teaspoons plain (all-purpose) flour
1 teaspoon Hungarian sweet paprika
½ teaspoon ground cinnamon
¼ teaspoon ground coriander
a large pinch of ground cloves
1 bay leaf
125 ml (4 fl oz/½ cup) hot chicken stock
2 tablespoons red wine vinegar
75 g (2½ oz/⅔ cup) walnuts, toasted and finely chopped
½ teaspoon soft brown sugar
2 large egg yolks

APPLE AND LINGONBERRY CRISPS

SERVES 6

125 g (4½ oz) unsalted butter

6 large granny smith or other crisp green apples, peeled, cored and diced

1½ tablespoons honey

2 teaspoons elderflower cordial

½ teaspoon finely grated lemon zest

315 g (11 oz/1 cup) lingonberry preserves

100 g (3½ oz/1¼ cups) fresh breadcrumbs made from light rye bread

1½ teaspoons ground cinnamon

½ teaspoon ground liquorice root

30 g (1 oz/⅓ cup) flaked almonds

45 g (1½ oz/¼ cup) soft brown sugar

Preheat the oven to 190°C (375ºC/Gas 5). Lightly grease six 250 ml (9 fl oz/1 cup) ramekins or similar-sized individual baking dishes or ovenproof cups.

Melt 2 tablespoons of the butter in a large frying pan over medium–high heat. Add the apple and sauté for 8–10 minutes, shaking the pan frequently until lightly golden. Add the honey, elderflower cordial and lemon zest and stir to combine. Remove from the heat and evenly divide the apple mixture between the prepared ramekins. Spoon 2 tablespoons of the lingonberry preserves over the apple in each ramekin and spread out with the back of a spoon.

To make the topping, combine the breadcrumbs, cinnamon, liquorice root, almonds and sugar in a bowl. Melt the remaining butter and pour into the breadcrumb mixture, stirring well to combine. Divide the breadcrumb mixture evenly over the top of the lingonberry preserves.

Place the ramekins on a tray and bake in the oven for 20–25 minutes, or until the tops are golden and crispy and the filling is heated through.

Serve with ice cream or sweetened whipped cream flavoured with a little vanilla.

COTTAGE CHEESE AND PLUM DUMPLINGS WITH CINNAMON WALNUTS

SERVES 6

Press the drained cottage cheese through a fine sieve into a bowl. Using beaters, cream together with the butter until smooth. Stir in the lemon zest, vanilla and egg yolks and then add the flours and the baking powder and mix to combine well. Cover and refrigerate for 30 minutes, or until firm.

Take ¼ cup of the mixture in the palm of your hand and flatten into a circle with a 6 cm (2½ inch) diameter. Place a heaped teaspoon of plum jam into the centre and cup your hand slightly so the dough starts to form a ball around the filling, then pinch the edges together with your other hand to seal in the filling, making sure there are no holes. Repeat with the remaining mixture to make twelve dumplings in total. Refrigerate until required.

Bring a very large saucepan of water to the boil and then add the oil and ½ teaspoon salt. Drop the dumplings into the boiling water one at a time, using a long spoon to carefully loosen any that stick to the bottom of the pot. When the water comes to the boil again, reduce it to a steady simmer and cook for 10 minutes, or until the dumplings rise to the surface. Lift out with a slotted spoon and place on a clean tea towel (dish towel) and drain well.

Meanwhile, heat the butter in a small frying pan over medium–high heat. Add the walnuts and cinnamon and cook for 4 minutes, stirring until the walnuts start to smell a little toasty — make sure the butter does not burn. Stir through the lemon juice.

Serve two dumplings per person with the walnut mixture spooned over the top and serve the icing sugar in a bowl on the side for people to sprinkle over as much as they like.

435 g (15¼ oz/1¾ cups) cottage cheese, well drained
2 tablespoons unsalted butter, softened
1 teaspoon finely grated lemon zest
½ teaspoon natural vanilla extract
2 large egg yolks
75 g (2½ oz/½ cup) plain (all-purpose) flour
60 g (2¼ oz/½ cup) potato flour
½ teaspoon baking powder
105 g (3½ oz/⅓ cup) thick European-style plum jam or plum preserves
60 ml (2 fl oz/¼ cup) vegetable oil

125 g (4½ oz) unsalted butter
85 g (3 oz/⅔ cup) finely chopped walnuts
1¼ teaspoons ground cinnamon
1 teaspoon freshly squeezed lemon juice
sifted icing (confectioners') sugar, to serve

CHOCOLATE FONDUE

SERVES 6–8

500 ml (17 fl oz/2 cups) pouring (whipping) cream, plus extra, to serve (optional)
200 g (7 oz) dark chocolate, very finely chopped
200 g (7 oz) milk chocolate Toblerone bars, very finely chopped
40 ml (1¼ fl oz) liqueur or schnapps, such as chocolate, cherry or almond (optional)

FOR DIPPING

seasonal fruit, sliced or whole if small, for dipping
cake or sweet bread, such as honeycake (see pages 216–17) or lebkuchen (see page 277), cubed (optional)
small marzipan balls (optional)
little pancakes (optional)
macaroons (optional)
marshmallows (optional)
pretzels (optional)

Set up your fondue pot following the manufacturer's instructions. Fill the pot with cream and heat over a medium flame until warm to the touch. Add both kinds of chocolate and stir constantly until the chocolate has melted and the mixture is very smooth and consistent in colour. Stir in the liqueur, if using.

Turn the flame off, pass around the fondue skewers and allow guests to take turns dipping their choice from a platter of various dipping ingredients in the chocolate mixture and drizzling over the extra cream if desired. If the chocolate starts to become too thick, you can relight the flame but keep on very low, stirring regularly. If the chocolate becomes grainy it has overheated. (If you prefer to play it safe, you can make the fondue half at a time.)

Serve with small glasses of the same liqueur you have flavoured the fondue with.

Note: If you don't have a fondue pot you can heat the cream in a small saucepan on the stove until just simmering, then remove from the heat and stir in the chocolate until melted, returning it to the stove over a low heat if needed. Take the pan to a heatproof mat on the table for serving, and if the chocolate begins to firm, return briefly to the stove over a low heat and stir until liquid again.

Variation: You can also flavour the fondue with spices — a nice wintry mix might include a good pinch of ground cinnamon, ginger and cardamom. You can also add a dash of natural vanilla or almond extract in place of the liqueur, if desired.

CHERRY STRUDEL

SERVES 10

DOUGH

225 g (8 oz/1½ cups) high protein flour or plain
  (all-purpose) flour, plus extra, for rolling
1 egg, lightly beaten
2 tablespoons vegetable oil
½ teaspoon cider vinegar

150 g (5½ oz) unsalted butter
160 g (5½ oz/½ cup) good-quality cherry jam
1½ tablespoons cherry schnapps or liqueur
2 teaspoons freshly squeezed lemon juice,
  strained
2 x 680 g (1 lb 8 oz) jars morello cherries,
  drained
80 g (2¾ oz/1 cup) fresh white breadcrumbs
55 g (2 oz/½ cup) ground almonds
45 g (1½ oz/¼ cup) soft brown sugar
1½ teaspoons ground cinnamon
icing (confectioners') sugar, for sifting

Sift the flour and a pinch of salt into a bowl and make a well in the centre. Combine the egg, all but 1 teaspoon of the oil and the vinegar and pour into the well with 2½ tablespoons of lukewarm water. Mix well until a soft dough forms, adding an extra teaspoon of water if required. Gather together and knead on a clean work surface for about 8 minutes, or until smooth and slightly elastic. Shape the dough into a ball and rub all over with the remaining oil. Put on a plate, cover with plastic wrap and leave to rest in a warm place for 2 hours.

Meanwhile, prepare the filling. Melt the butter in a saucepan over low heat and cook for 1 minute. Remove from the heat and sit for 5 minutes to allow to settle. Spoon off any foam from the surface and then pour the butter into a small, clean saucepan, making sure to avoid adding any of the sediment from the bottom of the first pan. Set aside until ready to use.

Combine the jam, schnapps and lemon juice in a bowl and stir until smooth. Add to the cherries and mix well. Cover and set aside. Combine the breadcrumbs, ground almonds, sugar and cinnamon in a separate bowl and set aside.

Preheat the oven to 190°C (375°F/Gas 5). After the dough has finished resting you can start the process of stretching it. You will need a large surface area to work on, such as a round table — about 1 x 1 metre (about 3¼ x 3¼ feet). Place a clean, fine cloth such as muslin (cheesecloth) over the top of your work area — it should be large enough to hang over two sides of your table. Tie a small weight, perhaps a teaspoon, to each corner to help weigh it down and then lightly sprinkle the surface of the cloth with the extra flour. Unwrap the dough and pull it into a round shape, about 15 cm (6 inches) in diameter. Place the dough in the centre of the cloth and lightly flour a sturdy rolling pin. Using strong, smooth strokes, roll out towards the edges of the cloth, working around the pastry but do not roll back over the area you have rolled — always roll outwards until you cannot roll it any further and the pastry is about 50 x 50 cm (20 x 20 inches).

Lightly flour your clean, jewellery-free hands and forearms. Carefully lift up the dough at the edge closest to you and slip your arms between the dough and the cloth, so that they are just under the centre of the dough circle.

Lift the dough off the table, ensuring the dough drapes evenly on either side. Now form your hands into fists and carefully stretch the dough by moving hand over hand outwards towards the edges of the dough. You will need to rotate the dough regularly so you stretch it evenly all over — this may take some practice and is easier if you enlist a friend to help!

When the dough has stretched about as far as you think it will go without tearing, and is about 60 x 60 cm (24 x 24 inches), place it back down onto the cloth. Carefully pull the dough out so that it is as wrinkle-free as possible. The dough should be almost transparent, however you may find that a few areas are a little thicker than others. If so, slip your hand underneath those patches and gently stretch them out so they are as thin as the rest of the dough. Trim the edges of the dough to form a rectangle-like shape. If your dough tears in places just pinch the edges together to seal it.

If needed, gently re-melt the butter you have set aside. With a long side of the pastry in front of you, brush two-thirds of the butter over the pastry and then sprinkle the breadcrumb mixture over the top, leaving a border of about 10 cm (4 inches) along the longer edges and 5 cm (2 inches) along each of the shorter edges.

Evenly spoon the cherry mixture on top of the breadcrumb mixture, just along the edge closest to you. Lightly brush the furthest edge from you with a little of the remaining butter. Using the cloth to help you, fold up the border of dough over the cherries and then carefully roll the strudel over twice. Fold in the two side edges and continue to roll up. Transfer the strudel to a large baking tray, seam side down. Keep the strudel straight, if possible, but if you find it is too long you can curve it gently to fit onto the tray. Brush the remaining melted butter over the top. Cook for 40 minutes, or until the pastry is crisp and golden. Remove from the oven, liberally sift icing sugar over the top and allow to rest for 15 minutes before cutting into thick slices. Serve warm with whipped cream or vanilla ice cream if desired.

Note: If you are in a hurry you can use long sheets of filo pastry instead of making this fiddly (but fabulous) dough. You will need to use about 8 layers of filo. The strudel will have a different texture, but will be delicious all the same!

QUARK FRITTERS WITH HONEY SYRUP

SERVES 6

Put the quark, cottage cheese, eggs, vanilla and sugar in a bowl and beat with electric beaters on high, until the mixture is smooth. Stir in the raisins and lemon zest and then sift over the flour and combine well. Cover with plastic wrap and refrigerate for 4 hours or overnight.

Use floured hands to roll heaped tablespoons of the mixture into balls and then flatten each into a 1 cm (½ inch) thick disc. Place on a baking tray lined with baking paper and repeat with the rest of the mixture to make eighteen discs in total.

Melt the butter and oil in a large heavy-based non-stick frying pan over medium–high heat. Cook the fritters, in batches, for 2 minutes on each side, or until golden. Drain on paper towels and keep warm in a low oven while you cook the remaining fritters.

Meanwhile, heat the honey, lemon juice and 1 tablespoon water in a small saucepan over medium–high heat until the honey is hot and runny. Serve the fritters with the honey syrup drizzled over the top and sour cream on the side, if desired.

Tip: These are great served with fresh or preserved fruits, such as apricots, cherries or figs.

Note: Quark, also known as qvark, is a fresh, soft white cheese from Central Europe. It is available from good delicatessens.

200 g (7 oz/1 cup) quark (qvark) or cream cheese (see note)
250 g (9 oz/1 cup) cottage cheese, well drained
2 large eggs
1 teaspoon natural vanilla extract
55 g (2 oz/¼ cup) caster (superfine) sugar
40 g (1½ oz/¼ cup) chopped raisins
¼ teaspoon very finely grated lemon zest
75 g (2½ oz/½ cup) plain (all-purpose) flour, plus extra, for coating
4 tablespoons unsalted butter
2 tablespoons vegetable oil
sour cream, to serve (optional)

HONEY SYRUP
175 g (6 oz/½ cup) honey
1 teaspoon freshly squeezed lemon juice

WARM CHOCOLATE AND WALNUT PANCAKE TORTE

SERVES 12

PANCAKES

300 g (10½ oz/2 cups) plain (all-purpose) flour

1 teaspoon baking powder

2 tablespoons icing (confectioners') sugar

4 large eggs

420 ml (14½ fl oz/1⅔ cups) full-cream (whole) milk

250 ml (9 fl oz/1 cup) pouring (whipping) cream

½ teaspoon natural vanilla extract

125 g (4½ oz) butter, melted

WALNUT FILLING

375 g (13 oz/3 cups) walnuts, toasted

330 ml (11¼ fl oz/1⅓ cups) pouring (whipping) cream

165 g (5¾ oz/1⅓ cups) icing (confectioners') sugar, sifted

2 teaspoons finely grated orange zest

3 tablespoons golden or dark rum

1 teaspoon instant coffee powder

1 teaspoon ground cinnamon

CHOCOLATE GLAZE

170 ml (5½ fl oz/⅔ cup) pouring (whipping) cream

100 g (3½ oz) dark chocolate, finely grated

50 g (1¾ oz) milk chocolate, finely grated

¼ teaspoon cornflour (cornstarch)

whipped cream, to serve

To make the pancakes, sift the flour, baking powder, icing sugar and a pinch of salt into a large bowl. Mix to combine and then make a well in the centre. Whisk together the eggs, milk, cream and vanilla and carefully pour into the well. Combine thoroughly and set aside to rest for 30 minutes.

Lightly brush a little melted butter over the base of a large non-stick frying pan and heat over medium–high heat until the butter starts to sizzle. Stir the batter well and ladle one-third of a cup of the mixture into the pan at a time, swirling to make a 20 cm (8 inch) pancake. Cook for 2 minutes on each side, or until lightly golden. Set aside and cover to keep warm while cooking the remaining batter — you should make about 16 pancakes in total. Brush the pan with butter every second pancake or so. (The first one or two are considered testers and can be discarded if they don't look as good as the rest.)

Meanwhile, finely grind 1 cup of the walnuts in a food processor. Finely chop the remaining walnuts and then place all the walnuts in a saucepan with the cream, icing sugar, orange zest, rum, coffee powder and cinnamon, and bring to the boil. Reduce the heat and simmer for 10 minutes, or until thickened but easily spreadable. Remove from the heat and cover to keep warm.

To make the chocolate glaze, heat the cream in a saucepan over medium heat until it just comes to the boil — remove from the heat and add both the chocolates, stirring well to combine. Combine the cornflour with 1 teaspoon of water to make a smooth paste and then stir into the chocolate. Return to medium heat and stir for 5 minutes, or until the chocolate has completely melted and the sauce has thickened slightly. Remove from the heat.

Meanwhile, place a pancake on a warmed serving platter and thinly spread with about 2 tablespoons of the walnut filling. Repeat with the remaining pancakes and walnut mixture, stacking them on top of each other as you go to create a layered cake. Don't spread the mixture on the last pancake — the final layer should be left plain. Pour half of the chocolate glaze over the top of the pancake stack and serve. Once at the table, cut it into thin wedges and dollop with whipped cream and the remaining chocolate glaze.

DIAMONDS AND FUR

BANISH THE BLEAK FROM THE LONGEST WINTER BY REVELLING IN THE GLAMOUR OF THE SEASON. DUST OFF THE FUR COAT AND CONJURE UP AN IMAGINARY PRIVATE JET RIDE WITH FRIENDS TO AN EXCLUSIVE ALPINE CHALET BESIDE THE PISTE, LIT ONLY BY TWINKLING LANTERNS AND THE REFLECTION OF AN OVERSIZED MOON. LUXURIATE IN MAGNUMS OF PREMIUM FIZZ AND DECADENTLY RICH CULINARY OFFERINGS THAT ARE PERFECT FOR ENTERTAINING — SIMPLY DIVINE!

GRILLED OYSTERS WITH CAULIFLOWER CUSTARD AND CAVIAR

SERVES 6

CAULIFLOWER CUSTARD

310 g (11 oz/2½ cups) cauliflower florets

125 ml (4 fl oz/½ cup) chicken stock

375 ml (13 fl oz/1½ cups) pouring (whipping) cream

1 garlic clove, chopped

½ brown onion, finely chopped

1 bay leaf

3 teaspoons bottled grated horseradish or horseradish relish

fine sea salt, to taste

white pepper, to taste

2 eggs

5 egg yolks

2 tablespoons vodka

2 teaspoons freshly squeezed lemon juice

1½ tablespoons melted butter

1 teaspoon caster (superfine) sugar

24 oysters, freshly shucked

good-quality caviar, to garnish

fine toasts, to serve

Put the cauliflower florets, stock, cream, garlic, onion and bay leaf into a saucepan and just bring to the boil. Reduce the heat, cover, and simmer for 15 minutes, or until the cauliflower is very tender. Remove the bay leaf and stir in the horseradish. Allow to cool slightly and then process the mixture in a food processor, in batches, until very smooth. Strain through a fine sieve, season to taste with the sea salt and a little white pepper, and cool slightly.

Preheat the oven to 160°C (315°F/Gas 2–3). Grease six 125 ml (4 fl oz/½ cup) moulds or ramekins and line the bottom of each with a circle of baking paper.

Whisk together the eggs and egg yolks, and then whisk them into the cauliflower cream. Season to taste. Pour the mixture into the prepared moulds and place them in a deep baking tray. Pour in enough warm water to come two-thirds of the way up the moulds, then cover the tray tightly with foil, piercing a couple of air holes in the top. Cook in the oven for 25 minutes, or until the custards are set but still slightly wobbly when tapped. Remove from the water bath and cool to room temperature. Carefully run a knife around the inside of each mould and invert onto the centre of a plate. Alternatively, you can serve the custards warm in the moulds, with a spoon.

Meanwhile, preheat the grill (broiler) to high. Combine the vodka, lemon juice, butter and sugar in a small bowl and divide between the oysters, spooning a little over each. Place the oysters on a tray and heat under the grill for 1½ minutes, or until lightly golden.

Place four oysters around each cauliflower custard. Garnish the custard with caviar and serve with the toasts.

BORLOTTI AND CHESTNUT SOUP WITH SCALLOPS AND PARSLEY OIL

SERVES 4

Using the point of a small knife, cut a small slit in the rounded stem end of each chestnut. Put them into a large saucepan, cover with cold water and bring to the boil over high heat. Cook for 15 minutes, then drain, cool slightly and peel.

Heat the butter in a saucepan over medium heat. Add the leek, celery and prosciutto and cook until softened. Add the chestnuts, borlotti beans, thyme sprig, garlic, apple, stock and 375 ml (13 fl oz/ 1½ cups) cold water. Bring to the boil over high heat, then reduce the heat and simmer for 40 minutes, or until the chestnuts and beans are very soft. Remove the thyme sprig and process the soup in a food processor, in batches, until smooth. Return the smooth soup to a clean saucepan and stir in the cream. Carefully reheat, making sure the soup does not boil; and season to taste. Keep the soup warm while preparing the scallops, or gently reheat when ready to serve.

Meanwhile, bring a small saucepan of water to the boil and add the parsley. Submerge for 1 minute, or until it turns bright green. Quickly transfer the parsley to iced water until cool and then shake off the excess water. Drain on paper towels and chop: Put the parsley into a food processor with the lemon zest, garlic, extra virgin olive oil and walnut oil and process until smooth; season to taste.

Heat a large frying pan over high heat. Put the scallops and olive oil in a small bowl and season with salt. Toss to combine. Cook the scallops for 1 minute on each side, or until golden and almost cooked through.

When ready to serve, ladle the warm soup into wide shallow bowls, top with three of the scallops and drizzle the parsley oil over the top. Serve immediately.

BORLOTTI AND CHESTNUT SOUP

300 g (10½ oz) fresh chestnuts

1 tablespoon butter

1 small leek, white part only, sliced

1 celery stalk, diced

50 g (1¾ oz) prosciutto, chopped

1 kg (2 lb 4 oz) fresh borlotti (cranberry) beans, peeled

1 thyme sprig

1 garlic clove, finely chopped

1 small granny smith apple, peeled, cored and grated

625 ml (21½ fl oz/2½ cups) chicken stock

125 ml (4 fl oz/½ cup) pouring (whipping) cream

PARSLEY OIL

2 large handfuls flat-leaf (Italian) parsley

¼ teaspoon finely grated lemon zest

1 garlic clove, crushed

170 ml (5½ fl oz/⅔ cup) extra virgin olive oil

2 teaspoons walnut oil

12 large white scallops, roe removed

1 tablespoon olive oil

DUCK LIVER AND TOKAJI MOUSSE WITH MUSCATELS AND WALNUT WAFERS

SERVES 8

450 g (1 lb) duck livers

500 ml (17 fl oz/2 cups) full-cream (whole) milk

200 g (7 oz) butter, diced

1 bacon slice, cut in half

4 French shallots, finely chopped

2 garlic cloves, finely chopped

1 teaspoon finely chopped thyme

1 bay leaf

1½ tablespoons Tokaji or Sauternes (see note)

¼ teaspoon freshly grated nutmeg

185 ml (6 fl oz/¾ cup) pouring (whipping) cream

fine sea salt, to taste

white pepper, to taste

16 very thin slices of day-old walnut bread, to serve

TOKAJI JELLY

500 ml (17 fl oz/2 cups) good-quality veal stock

250 ml (9 fl oz/1 cup) Tokaji or Sauternes (see note), plus 2 tablespoons extra

2 teaspoons cider vinegar

1 French shallot, finely chopped

1½ teaspoons powdered gelatine

1½ teaspoons sugar

thyme leaves, to garnish

Trim the duck livers of any sinew. Place in a non-metallic bowl, pour over the milk, cover and refrigerate overnight. Drain the livers when ready to use, discarding the milk.

Melt one-quarter of the butter in a frying pan over low heat and add the bacon, shallots, garlic, thyme and bay leaf. Cook for 8–10 minutes, or until the shallots are lightly golden. Remove from the heat and discard the bacon and bay leaf. Place the shallot mixture in the bowl of a food processor and add the Tokaji and nutmeg. Set aside.

Bring a saucepan of water to the boil. Add the drained duck livers and cook for 3–4 minutes, or until they have firmed up slightly but are still quite pink inside. Plunge them into iced water immediately to arrest the cooking process. Drain well and add to the food processor. Process until smooth, and then, with the motor still running, add the rest of the butter, a couple of pieces at a time, until all incorporated. Gradually pour in the cream and process until very smooth. Season to taste with salt and white pepper, then pass the purée through a fine sieve. Pour the mixture into eight 125 ml (4 fl oz/½ cup) ramekins or a 1 litre (35 fl oz/ 4 cup) mould. Cover with plastic wrap and refrigerate for at least 4 hours, or until firm to the touch.

To make the Tokaji jelly, place the stock, Tokaji, vinegar and shallots in a saucepan and bring to the boil. Reduce the heat and simmer for 45 minutes, or until reduced to 200 ml (7 fl oz). Strain into a bowl. Place the gelatine in a small bowl and whisk in 3 tablespoons of the hot liquid until the gelatine is dissolved, then stir it into the remaining liquid. Add the sugar and mix well. Cool to room temperature, stir in the extra Tokaji, and pour over the top of the firm mousse. Decorate with thyme leaves. Cover the moulds with plastic wrap and return to the fridge for 2 hours, or until the jelly has set.

While the jelly is setting, prepare the muscatels. Put the sprigs in a wide shallow bowl and add enough boiling water to cover. Set aside for 5 minutes, or until slightly softened, then drain. Put the sugar, Tokaji, vinegar, thyme sprig, orange zest and nutmeg in small frying pan over high heat and stir until the sugar has dissolved. Bring to the boil, then add the muscatel sprigs, and bring back to the boil. Reduce the heat and simmer for 5 minutes, or until the muscatels are starting to plump up and the liquid is syrupy. Remove from the heat, pour into a small bowl, and allow to cool completely. Discard the zest and thyme before serving.

To make the wafers, preheat the oven to 150°C (300°F/Gas 2). Place the slices of walnut bread in a single layer on a baking tray and cook in the oven for 5 minutes. Turn and cook for a further 3 minutes, or until dry and crisp.

Serve the mousse with the muscatels and walnut wafers on the side. Make sure you remove the mousse from the refrigerator 20 minutes before serving so it softens slightly.

Note: Tokaji is a sweet Hungarian wine and is best used in this dish, however Sauternes, a French dessert wine, is a good substitute.

Tip: If desired, serve the mousse with a small salad of baby beetroot (beet) greens dressed with a little walnut oil and orange juice.

MUSCATELS

8 small sprigs of dried muscatels on the vine (about 100 g/3½ oz)
2 tablespoons caster (superfine) sugar
60 ml (2 fl oz/¼ cup) Tokaji or Sauternes (see note)
2 teaspoons cider vinegar
1 very small thyme sprig
1 small strip orange zest, white pith removed
a pinch of freshly grated nutmeg

BUCKWHEAT BLINI PLATTER

SERVES 4–6

BLINI

10 g (¼ oz) fresh yeast
435 ml (15¼ fl oz/1¾ cups) lukewarm
  full-cream (whole) milk
90 g (3¼ oz/⅔ cup) buckwheat flour
200 g (7 oz/1⅓ cups) plain (all-purpose) flour
1½ teaspoons caster (superfine) sugar
2 eggs, separated
185 ml (6 fl oz/¾ cup) pouring (whipping)
  cream, whipped
butter, for cooking

CONDIMENTS

250 g (9 oz/1 cup) crème fraîche
2 hard-boiled eggs, yolks and whites separated
  and finely diced
200 g (7 oz) gravlax or smoked salmon
100 g (3½ oz) salmon roe
2 tablespoons finely chopped dill
½ handful chives, finely snipped
1 small red onion, very finely diced
Russian gherkins (pickles), finely diced
baby capers, rinsed and drained

Crumble the yeast into a bowl and pour over 3 tablespoons of the warm milk; mash until smooth. Mix in the remaining milk. Sift both of the flours into a bowl and then return the husks to the flour. Add the sugar and ½ teaspoon salt and stir to combine. Make a well in the centre, pour in the yeast mixture then mix in the egg yolks until smooth. Cover with plastic wrap and set aside in a warm place for 1 hour, or until the top of the mixture is covered in bubbles.

Whisk the egg whites to stiff peaks. Fold the whipped cream into the rested batter and then fold in the egg whites until well incorporated – be careful not to overmix or beat out all the air.

Melt a little butter in a large frying pan over medium–high heat. Drop 1½ tablespoons of the batter into the pan at a time, spreading them out slightly with the back of the spoon to form a circle with a 10 cm (4 inch) diameter. Cook for 1 minute, or until bubbles appear all over the top, then flip and cook for 1 minute on the other side. Transfer to a warmed plate and cover with a tea towel (dish towel) to keep warm while you cook the remaining batter — you should make about 18–20 blini in total.

Immediately serve the blini with all or a selection of condiments for guests to design their own blini toppings.

BALSAMIC-GLAZED VEAL SWEETBREADS WITH WHITE BEAN AND SAGE FRITTERS

SERVES 6

SWEETBREADS

500 g (1 lb 2 oz) veal sweetbreads (preferably
from milk-fed veal)

330 ml (11¼ fl oz/1⅓ cups) full-cream
(whole) milk

2 tablespoons freshly squeezed lemon juice,
strained

fine sea salt, to taste

seasoned plain (all-purpose) flour, for coating

3 tablespoons butter

1 tablespoon extra virgin olive oil

2 French shallots, very finely chopped

185 ml (6 fl oz/¾ cup) good-quality veal stock

3 tablespoons aged balsamic vinegar

2 teaspoons caster (superfine) sugar

1 large handful fresh sage leaves

1 large handful baby rocket (arugula) or other
baby greens (optional)

Place the sweetbreads in a non-metallic bowl and pour over enough milk to cover. Refrigerate for 6–8 hours and then drain, discarding the milk. Rinse the sweetbreads and then place in a saucepan with the lemon juice and sea salt, and cover with fresh cold water. Slowly bring to the boil over medium–high heat, then reduce the heat and simmer for 10 minutes, or until firm. Transfer the sweetbreads to a bowl of iced water until cool enough to handle. Carefully remove any membranes and excess fat but try to prevent the pieces from breaking up too much. Place on a baking tray lined with plastic wrap, cover with plastic wrap and then place another tray on top, weighing it down with several cans of food or similar weights. Refrigerate overnight.

To make the white bean fritters, place the cannellini beans, sage, garlic, lemon zest, flour, baking powder, egg, white pepper and sea salt in a food processor and process until very smooth — the texture should resemble a thick batter. Cover with plastic wrap and refrigerate for 1 hour.

Fill a deep-fryer or large, heavy-based saucepan one-third full of olive oil and heat to 180°C (350°F), or until a cube of bread dropped into the oil browns in 15 seconds. Using two spoons, shape heaped tablespoons of the mixture into quenelles and deep-fry, in batches, for 3–5 minutes each, turning occasionally until cooked through and golden. Drain on paper towels and keep warm in a low oven while you cook the sweetbreads. You should make about 18 fritters in total.

Cut lengthways through the centre of the sweetbreads to create two thinner sweetbreads. Lightly coat the sweetbreads with the seasoned flour. Melt half the butter with the oil in a large frying pan over medium–high heat. Fry the sweetbreads, in batches, for 3 minutes on each side, or until golden. Remove from the pan, cover to keep warm and set aside.

Add the remaining butter to the pan with the shallots and cook for a few minutes, or until softened and lightly golden. Add the stock and vinegar and cook for 4 minutes, or until it comes to the boil, making sure to scrape up any cooked–on bits from the bottom of the pan. Stir in the sugar, reduce the heat and simmer for 3–4 minutes, or until lightly glazy. Return the sweetbreads to the pan and turn to coat in the sauce.

Meanwhile, deep-fry the sage leaves for 30 seconds, or until crispy, and drain on paper towels.

Divide the sweetbreads among six large serving plates and place three fritters on each. Garnish with the crisp sage and serve with the rocket leaves on the side. Serve immediately.

WHITE BEAN FRITTERS

400 g (14 oz/2 cups) tinned cannellini beans, rinsed and drained well
3 teaspoons finely chopped fresh sage
3 garlic cloves, crushed
½ teaspoon finely grated lemon zest
1 tablespoon plain (all-purpose) flour
½ teaspoon baking powder
1 egg
⅛ teaspoon white pepper
1½ teaspoons sea salt
olive oil, for deep-frying

WHITE FISH PUDDING WITH PRAWN SAUCE

SERVES 6

WHITE FISH PUDDING

mild-flavoured olive oil, for brushing

700 g (1 lb 9 oz) skinless, boneless white fish
   fillets, such as cod or ling, chopped

310 ml (10¾ fl oz/1¼ cups) pouring (whipping)
   cream

1½ tablespoons cornflour (cornstarch)

2 eggs, separated

¼ teaspoon finely grated nutmeg

a large pinch of white pepper

1 teaspoon fine sea salt

1½ tablespoons chopped dill

dill sprigs, to garnish

Preheat the oven to 170°C (325°F/Gas 3). Brush a small straight-sided 25 x 9 cm (10 x 3½ inch) terrine tin (mould) with a little mild-flavoured oil and line the base and sides with baking paper so it hangs over the long sides.

To make the white fish pudding, put the fish fillets and cream in the chilled bowl of a food processor and process until smooth. Transfer to a bowl and whisk in the cornflour, egg yolks, nutmeg, white pepper, sea salt and chopped dill until well combined. Whisk the egg whites until firm peaks form and then mix a spoonful into the fish mixture. Carefully fold in the remaining egg white until well incorporated, being careful not to beat out too much air.

Pour the fish batter into the prepared tin and then tap firmly on the counter a couple of times to help remove any air bubbles. Fold the overhanging baking paper back over the top to cover the surface, then wrap tightly with foil. Set aside for 10 minutes to settle.

Place the terrine tin in a deep roasting tin and add enough hot water to come three-quarters of the way up the side of the terrine. Cook in the oven for 1½ hours, or until the top is firm and dry to the touch and a skewer inserted in the centre comes out clean.

Meanwhile, to make the prawn sauce, peel and de-vein the prawns, reserving the heads and shells, and then cover with plastic wrap and refrigerate until ready to use. Melt half of the butter in a large saucepan over medium–high heat. Add the prawn heads and shells and cook for 3 minutes, or until they turn bright orange. Remove from the pan and set aside.

Add the remaining butter, leek, carrot, celery, bay leaf and thyme sprig to the pan and cook over a low–medium heat for 10 minutes, or until the vegetables are lightly golden. Add the garlic and fennel seeds and cook for 1 minute, or until fragrant. Add the tomato paste and cook for 1 minute further, then add the Cognac, lemon zest and 1 litre (35 fl oz/ 4 cups) cold water and bring to the boil. Return the prawn heads and shells to the pan, reduce the heat and simmer for 30 minutes. Strain the liquid through a sieve into a clean saucepan. Discard the prawn heads and shells, thyme sprig and lemon zest but return the vegetable mixture to the liquid and simmer for a further 30 minutes, or until the liquid has reduced by half. Cool slightly, purée in a food processor, and then strain through a fine sieve. Place in a small saucepan, stir in the cream and season to taste. Bring to a simmer, then add the reserved prawns and cook for 3–4 minutes, or until the prawns are almost cooked through. Remove from the heat, cover, and set aside until ready to serve.

When the pudding is cooked, remove the terrine tin from the water bath and rest for 10–15 minutes before tipping out any excess liquid. After removing the foil and folding back the baking paper, carefully run a knife around the inside of the tin and gently invert. Cut into 6–8 thick slices and place each slice in the centre of a warmed wide, shallow bowl. Gently reheat the prawn sauce if needed and then ladle over the top, arranging three prawns on top of each pudding. Garnish with dill sprigs and serve immediately.

PRAWN SAUCE
18 raw medium king prawns
2 tablespoons butter
1 leek, white part only, finely sliced
1 carrot, finely chopped
1 celery stalk, finely chopped
1 bay leaf
1 small thyme sprig
1 garlic clove, finely chopped
½ teaspoon fennel seeds
1 tablespoon tomato paste (concentrated purée)
1½ tablespoons Cognac
1 small strip of lemon zest, white pith removed
1½ tablespoons pouring (whipping) cream

COTECHINO WITH PUMPKIN SFORMATO, CAVOLO NERO AND MUSTARD FRUIT DRESSING

SERVES 4

500 g (1 lb 2 oz) cotechino sausage

2 bunches cavolo nero (about 200 g/7 oz), chopped

1½ tablespoons olive oil

2 teaspoons butter

3 garlic cloves, finely sliced

a large pinch of freshly ground nutmeg

PUMPKIN SFORMATO

1 small butternut pumpkin (squash), unpeeled

1 brown onion, unpeeled

olive oil

1 teaspoon sea salt

1 tablespoon butter

¼ teaspoon freshly grated nutmeg

1 teaspoon very finely chopped sage

80 ml (2½ fl oz/⅓ cup) pouring (whipping) cream

25 g (1 oz/¼ cup) finely grated parmesan cheese

4 egg yolks

2 egg whites

Soak the sausage in a dish of cold water and refrigerate for 3–4 hours to remove some of the salt. Drain the sausage, then pierce all over with a thin skewer. Place in a large saucepan of cold water, bring almost to the boil over medium–high heat, then reduce the heat and simmer for 3 hours, or until very tender. Remove, cover, and set aside to rest for 20 minutes.

About halfway through cooking the sausage, make the sformato. Preheat the oven to 190°C (375°F/Gas 5). Cut the pumpkin into large chunks and halve the onion. Toss with a little olive oil and the sea salt in a roasting tin and cook in the oven for 1 hour, or until very tender. Reduce the oven temperature to 180°C (350°F/Gas 4). Remove the pumpkin and the onion from the oven, cool slightly, and then scoop the pumpkin and onion flesh into the bowl of a food processor or blender, discarding the skins. Process until smooth. Tip the pumpkin purée into a bowl and add the butter, nutmeg, sage and cream, stirring until the butter has melted. Allow to cool slightly, then stir through the parmesan and egg yolks and season, to taste. Whisk the egg whites until peaks form. Beat a spoonful of the egg white into the pumpkin mixture and then fold through the remaining egg white until it is thoroughly mixed in — be careful not to beat out all the air. Grease four 250 ml (9 fl oz/1 cup) ovenproof moulds or ramekins and divide the mixture between them, smoothing over the tops. Place in a deep baking dish and pour in enough warm water to come halfway up the sides of the moulds. Cook for 30 minutes, or until they are puffed and lightly golden.

Meanwhile, to make the mustard fruit dressing, whisk together the lemon juice, oil and mustard to combine, then stir through the mustard fruits and season to taste. Cover with plastic wrap and set aside until ready to serve.

Shortly before serving, bring a saucepan of water to the boil and add the cavolo nero. Cook for 4 minutes, or until wilted, and drain well. Heat the olive oil, butter, garlic and nutmeg in a large frying pan over medium–high heat until the garlic starts to become golden. Add the cavolo nero to the frying pan and toss to coat; season to taste. Keep warm.

Thickly slice the cotechino and pan-fry in a lightly oiled frying pan for 1–2 minutes on each side, or until lightly golden.

Serve the cotechino on a bed of cavolo nero and drizzle over the dressing. Serve with the warm pumpkin sformato on the side.

Tip: Adding some crunchy golden roast potatoes to this dish adds texture and helps to make it a substantial main course.

MUSTARD FRUIT DRESSING
1 tablespoon freshly squeezed lemon juice, strained
1½ tablespoons extra virgin olive oil
½ teaspoon dijon mustard
50 g (1¾ oz) mustard fruits, finely diced

SPICED DUCK BREAST WITH WALNUT-CRUSTED POTATO AND APPLE CROQUETTES AND CLOUDBERRY SAUCE

SERVES 4–6

4 x 200 g (7 oz) duck breast fillets
1 teaspoon ground coriander
1 teaspoon ground ginger
1 teaspoon ground aniseed
½ teaspoon ground cinnamon
a pinch of ground cloves
1 teaspoon fine sea salt

POTATO AND APPLE CROQUETTES

500 g (1 lb 2 oz) floury potatoes, cut into cubes
1 apple, peeled, cored and cut into large chunks
1 tablespoon butter
1 tablespoon sour cream
1½ tablespoons snipped chives
1 egg yolk, lightly beaten
plain (all-purpose) flour, for coating
2 eggs, lightly beaten
50 g (1¾ oz/½ cup) dry breadcrumbs
90 g (3¼ oz/¾ cup) finely chopped walnuts
vegetable oil, for deep-frying

Score several shallow slashes into the skin side of each duck breast. Rub the combined coriander, ginger, aniseed, cinnamon and cloves all over the breasts, then place in a non-metallic dish, cover with plastic wrap and refrigerate overnight.

To make the croquettes, put the potato and apple in a saucepan and cover with water. Bring to the boil and cook for 15 minutes, or until the potato is very tender. Drain well and mash with the butter and sour cream until smooth. Mix in the chives and egg yolk and season well. Cover with plastic wrap and refrigerate for 2 hours, or until cold and firm. Take heaped tablespoons of the mixture at a time and roll into croquette shapes. Working one at a time, lightly coat in the flour, then dip into the beaten egg, and finally roll in the combined breadcrumbs and walnuts, pressing to help it adhere. Place the croquettes in a single layer on a lined tray and refrigerate for at least 1 hour.

To make the cloudberry sauce, melt the butter in a small saucepan over medium–high heat. Add the onion and thyme and cook for 3 minutes, or until the onion is lightly golden. Add the jam, apple juice, vinegar and vodka and bring to the boil. Strain, discarding the solids, and return to the pan. Reduce the heat and simmer for 2 minutes, or until thickened to a glazy consistency. Set aside until ready to serve.

When ready to cook the duck, put a large heavy-based frying pan over a low–medium heat. Rinse the spices off the duck and pat dry with paper towels or a very clean tea towel. Rub the sea salt into the skin side of each breast, ensuring it gets into the slashes. Place the duck, skin side down, in the hot pan and cook for 12 minutes, or until most of the fat has rendered and the skin is golden. Remove from the pan and tip off all but 1 tablespoon of the fat. Increase the heat to medium–high, return the duck breasts to the pan, skin side up, and cook for 3 minutes to seal.

Increase the heat to high and turn the duck; cook for 2 minutes, or until the skin is crisp and dark golden. Rest for a few minutes before carving. The duck fat can be cooled and refrigerated to be used at a later date and is great for cooking potatoes.

While the duck is rendering, fry the croquettes. Fill a deep-fryer or a large heavy-based saucepan one-third full of oil and heat the oil to 180°C (350°F), or until a cube of bread dropped into the oil browns in 15 seconds. Deep-fry the croquettes, in batches, for 4 minutes each, or until golden and cooked through, turning occasionally to cook evenly on all sides. Keep the croquettes warm in a low oven while you cook the remainder.

Gently reheat the sauce if necessary. Slice the duck on a slight angle into three pieces and serve with the sauce spooned over and the croquettes on the side.

Tip: This dish is perfect with some wilted, dark, leafy greens such as spinach or kale.

CLOUDBERRY SAUCE
2 teaspoons butter
½ small brown onion, very finely diced
1 small thyme sprig
105 g (3½ oz/⅓ cup) cloudberry jam
60 ml (2 fl oz/¼ cup) fresh or good-quality
  bottled apple juice
1 tablespoon red wine vinegar
2 tablespoons vodka

BEEF WITH FOIE GRAS, SPICED COCOA SAUCE AND VANILLA-SCENTED BEANS

SERVES 4

SPICED COCOA SAUCE

2 teaspoons butter

2 French shallots, very finely diced

1 bay leaf

½ teaspoon white peppercorns

½ cinnamon stick

2 whole cloves

⅛ teaspoon caraway seeds

125 ml (4 fl oz/½ cup) verjus

750 ml (26 fl oz/3 cups) good-quality veal stock

10 g (¼ oz) bitter or dark chocolate, finely chopped

VANILLA-SCENTED BEANS

2 French shallots, very finely chopped

1½ tablespoons verjus

2 teaspoons sunflower oil

¼ vanilla bean, seeds scraped, bean reserved (see note)

a pinch of caster (superfine) sugar

200 g (7 oz) baby green beans

1 tablespoon butter

1 tablespoon sunflower oil

4 x 200 g (7 oz) beef fillets

4 x 1.5 cm (⅝ inch) thick slices of brioche, trimmed to match the beef

100 g (3½ oz) bloc de foie gras or a good-quality duck liver pâté

ground cocoa pods, to garnish (optional)

To make the spiced cocoa sauce, melt the butter in a saucepan over medium heat and add the shallots, bay leaf, peppercorns, cinnamon stick, cloves and caraway seeds. Cook for 3 minutes, or until the shallots have softened. Add the verjus and stock and bring to the boil. Reduce the heat and simmer for 25 minutes, or until the liquid has reduced by half. Strain, discarding the solids, and simmer again for 15 minutes, or until rich and slightly glazy. Remove from the heat and stir in the chocolate until melted and smooth. Set aside and cover to keep warm.

To make the vanilla-scented beans, combine all the ingredients in a bowl, except the beans. Bring a saucepan of water to the boil and cook the beans for 3 minutes or until just tender. Drain and toss with the dressing ingredients. Season to taste. Cover to keep warm.

Meanwhile, to cook the beef, heat half of the butter and half of the oil in a frying pan over high heat. Season the beef fillets and cook for 3 minutes on each side for a rare result. A further 1 minute or so each side will give you a medium result, however this will also depend on the thickness of the meat. Remove the meat from the pan and cover to keep warm while it rests for a few minutes. While the beef is resting, heat the remaining butter and oil in a clean frying pan over medium–high heat and cook the brioche slices for 1 minute on each side, or until golden.

Place a brioche slice on each plate and arrange a beef fillet on top. Slice the bloc de foie gras or pâté into four even pieces and lay a slice over the top of each beef fillet. Spoon over the spiced cocoa sauce, and sprinkle with a little ground cocoa pod, if using. Serve a small bundle of the beans on the side.

Note: If vanilla beans are placed in a jar of caster (superfine) sugar and allowed to infuse, a vanilla sugar is created, which is great for adding to sweet dishes and for coating doughnut balls (see pages 60–1).

POACHED VEAL WITH BEETROOT SPAETZLE AND HERBED CREAM

SERVES 6

BEETROOT SPAETZLE

225 g (8 oz/1½ cups) plain (all-purpose) flour
1 teaspoon fine sea salt
¼ teaspoon baking powder
2 eggs, beaten
125 ml (4 fl oz/½ cup) full-cream (whole) milk
6 large beetroot (beets), washed and cut in half

HERBED CREAM

375 ml (13 fl oz/1½ cups) pouring (whipping)
  cream
5 garlic cloves
1 bay leaf
1 thyme sprig
1 small marjoram sprig
1½ tablespoons finely chopped flat-leaf
  (Italian) parsley
1½ tablespoons finely snipped chives

To make the spaetzle, sift the flour, sea salt and baking powder into a bowl. Make a well in the centre and add the egg and half of the milk. Mix well to combine, gradually adding the remaining milk, until a firm but smooth dough forms — you may not need to add all the milk. Turn out onto a chopping board and roll to a 30 x 20 cm (12 x 8 inch) rectangle. Cover with plastic wrap and set aside.

To make the herbed cream, put the cream, garlic cloves, bay leaf and thyme and marjoram sprigs in a small saucepan and just bring to the boil. Reduce the heat and simmer for 10 minutes, or until the cream is reduced by half and the garlic has softened. Discard the bay leaf and thyme and marjoram sprigs and purée the cream mixture with the parsley and chives in a food processor until smooth. Return to a clean saucepan, cover, and set aside until needed.

To poach the veal, combine the stock, vinegar, thyme sprig, bay leaves, garlic and 500 ml (17 fl oz/2 cups) cold water in a large saucepan and bring to the boil over high heat. Cook for 5 minutes, then add the veal. Bring back to the boil, then reduce the heat, cover, and simmer for 20 minutes, turning occasionally. Turn off the heat but leave on the hotplate and allow to sit, covered, for 30 minutes for a nice pink result (allow to sit for a further 5–10 minutes longer if you prefer your meat a little more cooked). Transfer the veal to a plate and cover with foil to keep warm.

Meanwhile, juice the beetroot to make 500 ml (17 fl oz/2 cups). Put the juice and 250 ml (9 fl oz/1 cup) water in a large saucepan and bring to the boil. Place the chopping board with the dough on it in front of you so that the short ends are left and right. Starting 5 cm (2 inches) from the top edge of one long side, and working from left to right, use a large, sharp knife to mark out three horizontal lines at 5 cm (2 inch) intervals, resulting in four 5 cm (2 inch) wide horizontal strips.

Rest the edge of the chopping board on the side of the pot. Working quickly, dip a small palette knife into the beetroot juice and then scrape 5 mm (¼ inch) wide vertical strips off each marked horizontal strip of dough, straight from the board into the boiling liquid, continuing to dip the knife into the juice between each scrape. Only scrape off enough to cover the surface of the liquid and cook for 6–8 minutes, or until the spaetzle are tender and cooked through. Lift out with a slotted spoon into a bowl and cover to keep warm while cooking the remaining dough.

If necessary, gently reheat the herbed cream. Distribute the spaetzle between six large plates. Thickly slice the veal and rest on top and then spoon over the sauce. Garnish with some baby broad beans and serve immediately.

Note: Leftover cooking liquids can often be used for soups or stew bases. For example, try simmering some pelmeni (see pages 128–9) in this stock and serve as a dumpling soup.

1.5 litres (52 fl oz/6 cups) good-quality
  veal stock
185 ml (6 fl oz/¾ cup) red wine vinegar
1 large thyme sprig
2 bay leaves
4 garlic cloves, bruised
1.25 kg (2 lb 12 oz) veal nut, tied with string to
  hold its shape
95 g (3¼ oz/½ cup) blanched baby broad beans,
  to garnish (optional)

ROASTED ROSEMARY SQUAB WITH RED WINE AND CABBAGE RISOTTO

SERVES 4

Preheat the oven to 200°C (400°F/Gas 6). Rinse the squab inside and out and pat dry with paper towels. Put 1 rosemary sprig and 1 garlic clove into the cavity of each bird. Rub all over with olive oil and then season with sea salt. Place on a rack in a roasting tin, breast side up, and pour in 375 ml (13 fl oz/1½ cups) water. Roast in the oven for 12 minutes, or until the skin is just starting to colour. Reduce the temperature to 180°C (350°F/Gas 4) and cook for a further 25–30 minutes, or until golden all over and the juices run a pale pink colour when a skewer is inserted into the thickest part of the thigh. Remove from the oven, cover with foil and rest for 10 minutes.

About 10 minutes into the squab cooking time, make the risotto. Melt the butter and oil in a large saucepan over medium–high heat. Add the leek, carrot, celery and salami and cook for 10 minutes, or until the leeks are lightly golden. Add the rice and cook for 2 minutes, stirring constantly, until the rice becomes translucent. Stir in the garlic, tomato and cabbage and cook for 3–4 minutes, or until the cabbage just starts to wilt. Stir in the red wine and keep stirring until it has been absorbed into the rice. Add 125 ml (4 fl oz/½ cup) of the hot stock and stir continuously until the liquid has been absorbed. Continue adding the stock half a cup at a time, and stirring until it is all used, making sure the liquid has been absorbed before adding more — it should take about 20 minutes or so. Cover, remove from the heat and rest for a few minutes.

By now, the squab should have rested and the juices will be pooling in the roasting tin. Discard the rosemary and garlic. Carve the legs from each squab and then remove the breast from the bone and slice. Add any resting and carving juices to the rice with the butter, extra garlic and parmesan, and stir until the parmesan has melted. Season to taste. Divide the risotto between four wide shallow bowls. Arrange the squab on top, drizzle with a little balsamic glaze, if using, and garnish each dish with a rosemary sprig.

4 x 500 g (1 lb 2 oz) whole squab (pigeon), wing tips removed
4 rosemary sprigs, plus 4 extra, to garnish
4 large garlic cloves, bruised
olive oil
sea salt, to taste
balsamic glaze, for drizzling (optional) (see note)

RED WINE AND CABBAGE RISOTTO
1 tablespoon butter
1 tablespoon olive oil
1 leek, white part only, finely sliced
1 carrot, finely diced
1 celery stalk, finely diced
100 g (3½ oz) full-flavoured Italian salami, finely diced
330 g (11⅔ oz/1½ cups) risotto rice
1 garlic clove, very finely chopped, plus 1 clove extra, crushed
250 g (9 oz/1 cup) tinned chopped tomatoes
400 g (14 oz) cabbage, cut into 2 cm (¾ inch) squares
185 ml (6 fl oz/¾ cup) red wine
1 litre (35 fl oz/4 cups) hot chicken stock
2 tablespoons extra butter
25 g (1 oz/¼ cup) finely grated parmesan cheese

VENISON STROGANOFF WITH SWEET POTATO STRAWS

SERVES 4–6

SWEET POTATO STRAWS
2 white or orange sweet potatoes
vegetable oil, for deep-frying
sea salt, to taste

3 tablespoons butter
2 tablespoons olive oil
250 g (9 oz) French shallots, halved lengthways
250 g (9 oz) mixed seasonal mushrooms, such
  as Swiss brown, chantarelle, fresh porcini
  (cep) or pine mushrooms, sliced if large
3 garlic cloves, crushed
700 g (1 lb 9 oz) venison fillet, cut into 5 mm
  (¼ inch) thick slices
2 tablespoons brandy
250 ml (9 fl oz/1 cup) good-quality veal stock
1½ tablespoons tomato paste (concentrated
  purée)
2 teaspoons dijon mustard
½ teaspoon caster (superfine) sugar
a large pinch of ground allspice
160 g (5⅔ oz/⅔ cup) crème fraîche or Smetana,
  (see note, page 135)

To make the sweet potato straws, cook the whole sweet potatoes in boiling water for 15 minutes, or until just starting to become tender. Drain well and when cool enough to handle, peel and slice into very neat fine strips — about 6 cm (2½ inches) long and 5 mm (¼ inch) wide. Fill a deep-fryer or large heavy-based saucepan one-third full of oil and heat to 180°C (350°F). Deep-fry the potato straws, in batches, for 3–5 minutes each, or until crispy and golden. Drain on paper towels and season with sea salt. Keep warm in a low oven until ready to serve.

Meanwhile, heat half of the butter and half of the oil in a large heavy-based frying pan over medium–high heat. Add the shallots and cook for 5 minutes, or until lightly golden. Add the mushrooms and a pinch of salt, and sauté for 6–8 minutes, or until softened and lightly golden. Stir in the garlic and cook for a further 1 minute. Remove the mushrooms from the pan and set aside.

Add the remaining butter and oil to the pan and increase the heat to high. Toss the venison slices with a little salt and freshly ground black pepper. Working in small batches, quickly sear the slices of venison for 15 seconds on each side, or until nicely browned. Set aside. Reduce the heat to medium. Carefully stir in the brandy and stock, scraping up any cooked-on bits. Add the tomato paste, mustard, sugar and allspice and bring to the boil. Add a large spoonful of the hot liquid to the crème fraîche and whisk to combine, then add all the crème fraîche to the pan and stir well. Allow to simmer for 5 minutes, or until thickened slightly. Return the mushroom mixture to the pan and allow to gently reheat for a few minutes. Add the venison with any resting juices to the pan and turn to coat in the sauce. Season to taste and serve with the sweet potato straws on the side.

CAPER AND LEMON ROSTI-CRUSTED PERCH WITH CREAMED SPINACH AND LEEK

SERVES 4

Cook the whole potatoes in boiling water for about 12–15 minutes, or until just starting to become tender. Drain and set aside to cool.

Meanwhile, to make the creamed spinach and leek, place the leaves in a colander and pour boiling water over the spinach to wilt thoroughly. When cool enough to handle, squeeze tightly to extract any excess liquid, chop and set aside.

Melt the butter in a frying pan over medium heat and add the leek. Cook for 8 minutes, or until softened, but do not allow to brown. Stir in the garlic and nutmeg and cook for 1 minute. Sprinkle the flour over the leek mixture and stir through for 1 minute. Add the crème fraîche and lemon juice and mix well to combine. Stir in the chopped spinach and season to taste. Cover and set aside until ready to serve.

When the potatoes are cool, peel and coarsely grate them into a bowl. Add the lemon zest, capers and chives and season to taste, stirring well to combine.

Lightly coat the fish fillets in flour, then dip one side in the egg and allow any excess to drip off. Evenly press one-quarter of the potato mixture onto the egg-coated surface of each fish fillet and refrigerate for 10 minutes to help set.

Heat the butter and oil in a large non-stick frying pan over medium–high heat. When the butter is sizzling, carefully add the fish fillets, potato side down, and cook for 8 minutes, or until the potato side is golden and crisp. Carefully insert a metal spatula underneath the fish and turn over; cook for 2–4 minutes, or until lightly golden and just cooked through — the exact cooking time will vary depending on the thickness of the fish fillets.

Gently reheat the creamed spinach and leek, if necessary, and divide between four warmed plates. Place the fish on top and serve with a lemon wedge for squeezing over.

Variation: Snapper fillets may be used in place of perch.

2 large all-purpose potatoes, such as desiree, unpeeled
¼ teaspoon very finely chopped lemon zest
1½ tablespoon baby capers, rinsed, drained and finely chopped
1½ tablespoons finely snipped chives
4 x 180 g (6¼ oz) skinless, boneless perch fillets
plain (all-purpose) flour, for coating
1 egg, lightly beaten
3 tablespoons butter
2 tablespoons sunflower oil or other mild-flavoured oil
lemon wedges, to serve

CREAMED SPINACH AND LEEK
500 g (1 lb 2 oz) English spinach leaves
2 tablespoons butter
1 large leek, white part only, sliced
1 garlic clove, crushed
½ teaspoon freshly grated nutmeg
1½ teaspoons plain (all-purpose) flour
185 g (6½ fl oz/¾ cup) crème fraîche
2 teaspoons freshly squeezed lemon juice

LIQUORICE LAMB WITH ROASTED FENNEL AND CARROTS, HAVARTI CREAM AND SWEET CARROT JUS

SERVES 4

To make the carrot jus, heat the oil in a large saucepan over medium–high heat and brown the bones well — you may need to do this in batches. Return all the bones to the pan with the onion, bay leaf, carrot juice, orange zest, cumin, honey and 1 litre (35 fl oz/4 cups) cold water. Bring to the boil, then reduce the heat to a rapid simmer and cook for 1 hour, or until the liquid has reduced by half, skimming regularly to remove any scum from the surface. Strain into a smaller saucepan, return to the heat and continue to cook for a further 50 minutes, or until the liquid is slightly glazy and reduced to about 185 ml (6 fl oz/¾ cup). Set aside and cover to keep warm.

About an hour before the end of the jus cooking time, preheat the oven to 180°C (350°F/Gas 4). Cut the fennel bulb into 16 thin wedges, reserving the fronds. Put the fennel and carrots in a roasting tin, drizzle with the olive oil, sprinkle with the sea salt and toss to coat. Cook for 15 minutes, or until the fennel starts to become tender. Dollop the butter over the vegetables and continue cooking for 10 minutes, or until the vegetables are tender and lightly golden.

Meanwhile, to make the havarti cream, put the cream, potato and garlic in a saucepan over medium–high heat for about 4–5 minutes, or until the cream is just about to boil. Reduce the heat and simmer for 5 minutes. Using a fork, crush the potato into the cream until smooth. Stir in the havarti until it has melted and the mixture is smooth and thick. Cover and set aside until ready to serve.

When ready to cook the lamb, combine the grated liquorice root and sea salt and sprinkle all over the lamb pieces. Use your fingers to rub the seasonings into the meat. Heat the oil in a large heavy-based frying pan over medium–high heat. Add the lamb and cook on one side for 3–4 minutes, or until well browned, and then turn and cook the other side for 3–4 minutes for a pink result. Remove from the pan, cover and rest for about 5 minutes and then carve each piece of lamb into three slices on an angle.

Divide the havarti cream over the base of four warmed serving plates. Divide the roasted vegetables over the top. Decoratively place the lamb over the vegetables and drizzle over the carrot jus. Garnish with a few of the reserved fennel fronds and serve immediately.

CARROT JUS
2 teaspoons olive oil

1 kg (2 lb 4 oz) lamb bones

1 small brown onion, chopped

1 bay leaf

500 ml (17 fl oz/2 cups) fresh carrot juice, strained (approximately 12 carrots)

½ teaspoon finely grated orange zest

½ teaspoon ground cumin

1 tablespoon honey

ROASTED FENNEL AND CARROTS
1 large fennel bulb, with feathery fronds

12 baby carrots

2 tablespoons olive oil

sea salt

20 g (¾ oz) butter

HAVARTI CREAM
310 ml (10¾ fl oz/1¼ cups) pouring (whipping) cream

1 small floury potato, peeled cooked and finely diced

1 garlic clove, crushed

120 g (4¼ oz/1 cup) grated havarti cheese

3 teaspoons finely ground liquorice root

1 teaspoon fine sea salt

4 x 200 g (7 oz) lamb backstraps (loin), trimmed of excess fat

olive oil, for pan-frying

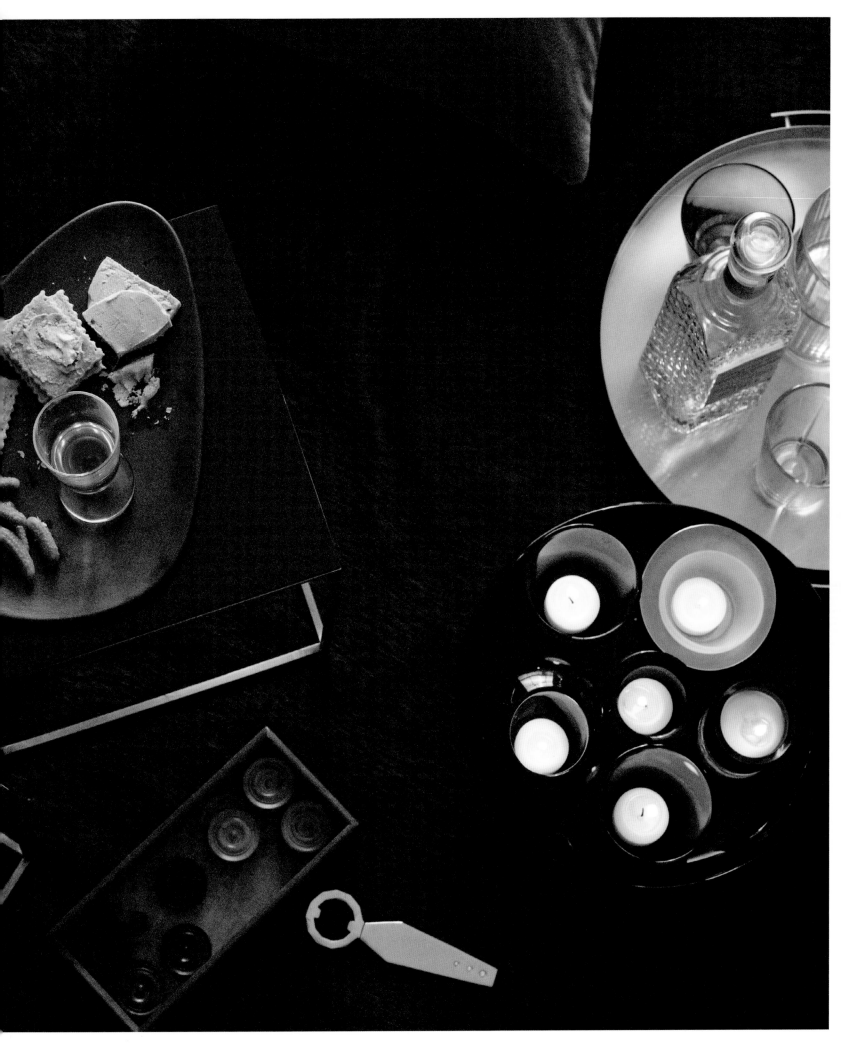

VEAL CUTLETS WITH WHEAT BEER SAUCE AND WINTER VEGETABLE STRUDEL

SERVES 4

WINTER VEGETABLE STRUDEL
1 floury potato
1 small swede (rutabaga)
1 carrot
75 g (2½ oz/1 cup) shredded cabbage
3 tablespoons butter, melted
1 garlic clove crushed
1 teaspoon finely chopped sage
1 large handful flat-leaf (Italian) parsley,
   finely chopped
1 handful chives, snipped
1 sheet frozen puff pastry
125 g (4½ oz) goat's curd
1 egg, lightly beaten

WHEAT BEER SAUCE
125 ml (4 fl oz/½ cup) wheat beer
2 tablespoons dried muscatels or raisins
250 ml (9 fl oz/1 cup) good-quality veal stock
2 tablespoons honey
1 small sage sprig

olive oil, for pan-frying
4 x 250 g (9 oz) thick veal cutlets

To make the vegetable strudel, peel the potato, swede and carrot and thinly slice using a mandolin or a very sharp knife. Bring a large saucepan of water to the boil and add the sliced vegetables and the cabbage. Allow to come to the boil again and cook for 10–12 minutes, or until the potato is tender. Drain well and cool slightly before placing in a bowl with half of the butter, the garlic, sage and half of both the parsley and chives. Season well and toss to combine, breaking up any larger pieces with the edge of a spoon. Allow to cool completely.

Preheat the oven to 210°C (415°F/Gas 6–7). Place the sheet of puff pastry on your work surface and roll it out to a thickness of 1 mm. The short sides should be left and right. Evenly spread the goat's curd over the pastry leaving a 5 cm (2 inch) border on two long sides and a 2 cm (¾ inch) border on each short side. Sprinkle the remaining parsley and chives over the goat's curd and then neatly spoon the vegetable mixture on top of that, pressing down lightly. Brush some egg around the border and roll up from the bottom edge to form a log, tightly pressing the edges and pinching the sides to seal. Place the strudel, seam side down, onto an oven tray lined with baking paper. Brush the strudel with the remaining melted butter. Bake in the oven for 30 minutes, or until the pastry is golden and crisp. Remove and allow to rest for 6–8 minutes.

Meanwhile, make the beer sauce by placing the wheat beer, muscatels, stock, honey and sage sprig in a small saucepan. Bring to the boil, then reduce the heat and simmer for 15 minutes, or until the sauce has thickened to a coating consistency. Remove the sage sprig, season to taste, and cover to keep warm while you cook the cutlets.

Heat the oil in a large, heavy-based frying pan over medium–high heat. Season the veal on both sides and then cook on each side for about 4 minutes. Remove from the heat, cover and set aside for 5 minutes. Stir any resting juices into the sauce and reheat gently if necessary.

Drizzle the sauce over the cutlets and serve with a slice of strudel on the side.

POT AU FEU

SERVES 8

Put the beef short ribs, sausages, bacon, garlic, onion, carrot, celery, bay leaves and thyme in a large saucepan and pour over 4 litres (140 fl oz) cold water. Bring just to the boil, then reduce the heat and simmer for 30 minutes, skimming off any scum from the surface. At this stage, remove the sausages, transfer them to a large bowl and refrigerate while you continue cooking. Cook the stew for a further 2–2½ hours, or until the other meats are very tender. Transfer all the meats to the bowl with the sausages and strain the liquid over them — discard all the solids from the sieve except the onion, which you can return to the meats. Cool slightly, cover and refrigerate overnight.

The next day, carefully spoon off all the solidified fat from the surface and put the meats and their cooking liquid into a large saucepan with the leek, celeriac, turnips, carrots and Champagne and bring just to the boil. Reduce the heat and simmer for 15 minutes, or until the vegetables are tender.

Meanwhile, if using, wrap the pieces of marrow bone in muslin (cheesecloth) and tie with kitchen string — this is to keep the marrow from coming out of the bones. Place in a saucepan with 1 teaspoon of salt, then cover with cold water and bring to the boil. Reduce the heat and simmer for 20 minutes. Turn off the heat and keep in the pan until ready to serve.

When the meat and vegetables are ready, remove from the heat and take all the meat out of the broth. Thickly slice the sausages and cut the bacon into eight pieces. Place it all onto a large, warmed serving platter, keeping the sausage separate. Lift the vegetables out of the broth and add to the serving platter. Spoon a little broth over the meats and vegetables to keep them moist and then cover to keep warm.

Unwrap the marrow bones, scoop out the marrow and smear onto the baguette toasts. Add the parsley to the broth in the pot, season to taste, and ladle into individual bowls. Serve this as a first course with the toasts, followed by the platter of meats and one or more of the accompaniments. You can also serve it with some boiled baby potatoes, if desired.

2 kg (4 lb 8 oz) beef short ribs, cut into 5 cm (2 inch) pieces, trimmed of excess fat
4 thick French-style pork sausages, pricked all over
300 g (10½ oz) whole piece streaky bacon
4 garlic cloves
1 onion, peeled and studded with 4 cloves
1 carrot, roughly chopped
1 celery stalk, roughly chopped
2 bay leaves
1 large thyme sprig
2 leeks, white part only, cut into four pieces
1 celeriac, diced
8 baby turnips or 2 turnips, cut into wedges
16 baby carrots
125 ml (4 fl oz/½ cup) Champagne
8 pieces of marrow bone (optional)
8 thin slices of baguette, lightly toasted
1 large handful flat-leaf (Italian) parsley, very finely chopped

ACCOMPANIMENTS
cornichons
grated horseradish
djion mustard
aioli
gourmet salt, such as fleur de sel

BEEF FILLET IN PARMESAN PASTRY WITH TRUFFLE BUTTER SAUCE

SERVES 8

PARMESAN PASTRY
375 g (13 oz/2½ cups) plain (all-purpose) flour
150 g (5½ oz) cold butter, diced
60 g (2¼ oz/⅔ cup) finely grated parmesan
  cheese
1 egg
3 tablespoons full-cream (whole) milk

2 tablespoons butter
1 brown onion, finely chopped
200 g (7 oz) fresh porcini (cep) or other
  seasonal mushroom, thinly sliced
1 garlic clove, crushed
½ teaspoon finely chopped rosemary
20 g (¾ oz/¼ cup) day-old white breadcrumbs
1 large handful flat-leaf (Italian) parsley,
  chopped
2 tablespoons olive oil
1.6 kg (3 lb 8 oz) beef fillet (ask your butcher
  for a cut from the centre of the fillet so it is
  an even thickness all over)
1 small egg, beaten

To make the pastry, sift the flour into a food processor. Add the butter and parmesan and pulse until it resembles breadcrumbs. Add the egg and 2 tablespoons of the milk and process until the mixture just comes together to form a soft dough, adding the remaining milk if needed. Gather the pastry into a ball and flatten it into a disc. Cover with plastic wrap and refrigerate for at least 2 hours.

Melt the butter in a large, heavy-based frying pan over medium-high heat. Add the onion and cook for 5 minutes, or until softened. Add the mushroom, garlic and rosemary and cook for 8 minutes, or until the mushrooms have softened. (Depending on the type of mushroom used and its freshness there may be some juices released, if so, continue cooking for an extra few minutes or until the liquid has evaporated.) Transfer the mushroom mixture to a bowl, stir in the breadcrumbs and parsley, and season to taste. Set aside and allow to cool completely.

Return the frying pan to high heat. Rub the olive oil all over the beef and season with salt and freshly ground black pepper. Brown the meat for 8–10 minutes, turning every 2 minutes to seal on all sides and brown all over. Remove the beef from the pan and allow to cool.

Preheat the oven to 190°C (375°F/Gas 5). Remove the pastry from the refrigerator and sit for 10 minutes at room temperature to soften slightly, then roll out on a lightly floured surface into a large rectangular shape, about 50 x 35 cm (20 x 14 inches). Trim all the edges to neaten the rectangle. Spoon the mushroom mixture lengthways along the top of the pastry, about 8 cm (3¼ inches) from the edge — the mushroom mix should spread out to be roughly the same length and width as the beef. Sit the beef on top. Brush along the parallel long edge of the pastry and the two short ends with a little egg. Roll the pastry over the beef to overlap the edges and press to seal, making sure the pastry is firmly against the meat. Fold in the ends and pinch the edges together.

Place the roll on a greased oven tray, seam side down. If you like, you can make decorations from the pastry scraps to stick on the top of the pastry before you brush it all over with the remaining egg. Make a couple of small air vents in the top of the pastry with the tip of a sharp knife. Cook in the oven for 35–40 minutes on the bottom shelf for a rare result; an extra 5–8 minutes will result in medium–rare. If the pastry is browning too quickly, loosely cover with foil. Remove from the oven, cover and set aside to rest for 10–15 minutes.

While the beef is cooking, make the sauce. Put the wine, vinegar, shallots, peppercorns, and parsley and rosemary sprigs in a saucepan. Bring to the boil, then reduce the heat and simmer for 15 minutes, or until reduced to about 2 tablespoons. Strain into a heatproof bowl and cool slightly. Beat in the egg yolks and then place over a saucepan of simmering water, ensuring the water does not touch the base of the bowl, and whisk for 1–2 minutes, or until thickened slightly. Whisk in the butter, a few cubes at a time, adding more only after each piece is well combined. When done, the sauce should be thick and glossy. Remove from the heat, stir in the chopped truffle and the truffle oil, if desired, for extra flavour. Season to taste.

Once the meat has rested, cut the ends of the pastry and discard, then cut the beef roll into eight slices. Serve with the sauce on the side for spooning over

Tip: Serve with lightly cooked greens and some boiled baby potatoes.

TRUFFLE BUTTER SAUCE
185 ml (6 fl oz/¾ cup) pinot grigio
80 ml (2½ oz/⅓ cup) white wine vinegar
4 French shallots, finely chopped
½ teaspoon white peppercorns
3 parsley sprigs
1 small rosemary sprig
4 large egg yolks
220 g (7 oz) butter, diced and chilled
1 small black truffle, very finely chopped
a few drops of truffle oil (optional)

JUNIPER-DUSTED VENISON FILLET WITH GJETOST SAUCE AND BEETROOT RELISH

SERVES 4

BEETROOT RELISH

55 g (2 oz/¼ cup) caster (superfine) sugar
2 teaspoons butter
2 French shallots, very finely chopped
2 tablespoons red wine vinegar
2 tablespoons red wine
1 small thyme sprig
3 juniper berries
1 cooked beetroot (beet), finely diced

GJETOST SAUCE

250 ml (9 fl oz/1 cup) good-quality veal stock
1 garlic clove, bruised
1 small thyme sprig
60 ml (2 fl oz/¼ cup) pouring (whipping) cream
60 g (2¼ oz) gjetost, grated (see note)

2 kohlrabies
vegetable oil
1½ teaspoons sea salt, plus extra to serve
2 teaspoon ground juniper berries
800 g (1 lb 12 oz) whole venison fillet
1 tablespoon butter
1 tablespoon oil

To make the beetroot relish put the sugar and 2 tablespoons water in a saucepan over high heat and stir until the sugar dissolves. Bring to the boil and cook, without stirring, for 5–7 minutes, or until golden. Remove from the heat and carefully add the butter, shallots, vinegar, red wine, thyme sprig and juniper berries. Bring to the boil again, then add the beetroot and 250 ml (9 fl oz/1 cup) water. Reduce the heat and simmer for 25 minutes, stirring often, until the liquid has almost evaporated. Remove and discard the juniper berries and thyme sprig. Set the relish aside until needed.

Preheat the oven to 190°C (375°F/Gas 5). To make the sauce, put the stock, garlic and thyme sprig into a saucepan and bring to the boil. Reduce the heat and simmer for 8–10 minutes, or until reduced to 80 ml (2½ fl oz/⅓ cup). Remove the garlic and thyme. Stir in the cream, and cook over medium heat for a further 2 minutes, or until slightly thickened. Stir in the gjetost until melted and smooth; season to taste. Remove from the heat, cover and set aside.

Peel the kohlrabies, then cut each in half. Trim off the rounded sides of each half so you end up with two thick, flat discs from each vegetable. Trim off any rough edges to neaten. Place on a baking tray, brush with vegetable oil and sprinkle with a little sea salt. Cook in the oven for 50 minutes, or until lightly golden and tender when pierced.

Meanwhile, mix 1½ teaspoons freshly ground black pepper with the sea salt and ground juniper berries, crushing the salt with the back of a spoon. Rub the spice mix all over the venison. Heat the butter and oil in a frying pan over medium–high heat and when hot, sear the venison well on all sides — about 2 minutes on each side. Remove from the pan and place on a baking tray.

Add the venison to the oven in the last 25 minutes of the kohlrabies' cooking time for a rare result — you can add it 5 minutes earlier if you prefer it a little more cooked. Remove from the oven, lightly cover with foil, and set aside to rest for 10–15 minutes. Gently reheat the gjetost sauce, if necessary.

Trim the very ends off the venison fillet, then cut the remainder into eight even slices. Place a piece of kohlrabi on each plate and top with 2 slices of venison, one slightly overlapping the other. Spoon a little of the beetroot relish on top of the veal and spoon the gjetost sauce around the vegetable. Serve some lightly cooked greens on the side, and maybe some potato and apple croquettes (see pages 186–7) or potato and cabbage cakes (see pages 248–9).

Note: Gjetost is a sweet, caramel coloured cheese from Norway. It is usually served thinly sliced on crispbreads — there is no real substitute as it is quite unique. It is available at large supermarkets and good delicatessens.

SALMON WITH RED WINE SAUCE ON SAUTEED CABBAGE AND SPECK

SERVES 4

To make the red wine sauce, melt the butter in a saucepan over medium–high heat and add the shallots and cloves. Cook for 8 minutes, or until the shallots are softened and golden. Add the wine, speck, bay leaf, carrot, celery and 250 ml (9 fl oz/1 cup) water and bring to the boil. Reduce the heat and simmer for 10 minutes, or until the liquid is reduced to about 125 ml (4 fl oz/½ cup). Strain into a clean saucepan and return to a simmer. Mash together the flour and butter until smooth, then whisk into the sauce, a little at a time, until the sauce becomes slightly thickened and glossy. Season to taste and set aside until ready to serve.

To cook the cabbage, melt the butter in a large frying pan over medium–high heat. Add the onion and speck and cook for 10 minutes, or until the onion is softened and lightly golden. Add the garlic, cabbage and 80 ml (2½ fl oz/⅓ cup) water with a pinch of salt, and cook for 15 minutes, or until the cabbage is wilted and tender but still has a little crunch. Stir through the parsley, then remove from the heat and keep warm until ready to serve.

Meanwhile, place a large non-stick frying pan over high heat. Rub the salmon fillets with a little oil to coat. Season the skin side with salt and freshly ground black pepper and cook, skin side down, for 4–5 minutes, or until the skin is crispy. Turn over and cook the other side for 2–3 minutes for a medium result or a little longer if you like your salmon well cooked — the exact time will depend on the thickness of the fillets. Serve the salmon fillets, skin side up, on a bed of the cabbage mixture and drizzle with a little of the red wine sauce.

Note: You can use monkfish fillets in place of salmon if you prefer a meaty white fish.

RED WINE SAUCE

1 tablespoon butter
3 French shallots, finely chopped
a small pinch of ground cloves
375 ml (13 fl oz/1½ cups) red wine, ideally German Spatburgunder or pinot noir
20 g (¾ oz) speck, finely diced
1 bay leaf
½ small carrot, finely diced
½ celery stalk, finely diced
½ teaspoon plain (all-purpose) flour
1 teaspoon butter

SAUTEED CABBAGE AND SPECK

2 tablespoons butter
1 red onion, finely sliced
60 g (2¼ oz) speck, finely diced
1 garlic clove, finely sliced
½ savoy cabbage, finely shredded
1 handful flat-leaf (Italian) parsley, chopped

4 x 200 g (7 oz) salmon fillets, skin on
sunflower oil, for pan-frying

HONEYCAKE SNOWBALLS WITH FIG AND BUTTERED RUM SAUCE

SERVES 8

GINGER ICE CREAM

1 tablespoon ground ginger

½ vanilla bean, split

375 ml (13 fl oz/1½ cups) full-cream
(whole) milk

250 ml (9 fl oz/1 cup) pouring (whipping) cream

5 egg yolks

115 g (4 oz/½ cup) caster (superfine) sugar

1 tablespoon honey

2 teaspoons Bärenjäger or European
honey liqueur

FIG SAUCE

8 good-quality whole dried dessert figs

60 ml (2 fl oz/¼ cup) dark rum

60 ml (2 fl oz/¼ cup) boiling water

60 g (2¼ oz/⅓ cup) soft brown sugar

2 tablespoons unsalted butter

walnut halves, toasted

2 teaspoons Bärenjäger or European
honey liqueur

To make the ice cream, put the ginger, vanilla bean, milk and cream in a saucepan over medium–high heat and bring almost to the boil. Reduce the heat and simmer for 5 minutes. Remove from the heat and set aside for 20 minutes for the flavours to infuse. Meanwhile, whisk together the egg yolks, sugar and honey until thick and creamy.

Gently reheat the cream mixture, then gradually whisk into the egg yolks until smooth. Place over a low–medium heat and cook for 10 minutes, stirring continuously, until the custard easily coats the back of a spoon. Cool slightly and strain into a bowl. Stir in the liqueur, cover with plastic wrap, and refrigerate until cold. Churn in an ice-cream machine according to the manufacturer's instructions. Alternatively, you can transfer to a shallow metal tray and freeze, whisking every couple of hours until frozen and creamy. Freeze until ready to use.

To make the sauce, put the figs and rum in a bowl and pour over the boiling water. Allow to sit for 1 hour, or until the figs have softened. Cut the figs into small dice. Combine the sugar and butter in small saucepan with 60 ml (2 fl oz/¼ cup) water and stir over high heat until the sugar has dissolved. Bring to the boil and boil for 8 minutes, or until thick and glossy. Add the figs, then remove from the heat and set aside until ready to use.

Preheat the oven to 180°C (350°F/Gas 4). To make the cake, put the butter, sour cream, sugar and honey in a large bowl and beat with electric beaters on high for 10 minutes, or until pale and creamy. Add the eggs, one at a time, beating well after each addition. Sift the flour, baking powder and spices together, then fold into the batter. Lightly grease 10 non-stick 125 ml (4 fl oz/½ cup) muffin holes, then divide the batter between the holes, only filling them three-quarters full. Cook on the middle shelf of the oven for 20–25 minutes, or until a skewer comes out clean when inserted into the centre. Cool completely in the tin.

To make the soft meringue topping, combine the sugar with 2 tablespoons water in a saucepan over high heat and stir until the sugar has dissolved. Bring to the boil and boil for 6–7 minutes, or until a soft ball forms when a little of the mixture is dropped into a glass of cold water — you should be able to squish it between your fingers. Meanwhile, whisk the egg whites with electric beaters until frothy, then add the cream of tartar and continue whisking until soft peaks form. Slowly add the boiling syrup while you continue to beat on high speed, then once all the syrup is added, continue beating for 6–8 minutes, or until very thick and cool to the touch.

Remove the cakes from the tin and scoop out the centre of each cake, leaving a 1 cm (½ in) rim or border around the top of each cake to make a hole that will fit a scoop of the ice cream.

Put a scoop of ginger ice cream inside each hole and place directly into the freezer as you are working, so the ice cream doesn't melt. Working quickly, remove one cake from the freezer at a time and cover the tops and sides with the meringue topping, then spike and swirl the meringue to resemble a snowball. Return to the freezer as you finish each one.

Gently reheat the sauce, adding the walnuts and liqueur. Place each snowball onto a plate and spoon some of the sauce around. Serve immediately.

Note: This recipe makes ten honeycakes, allowing for breakages when filling and will serve 8 people.

HONEYCAKE

150 g (5½ oz) unsalted butter, softened
90 g (3¼ oz/⅓ cup) sour cream
115 g (4 oz/½ cup) soft brown sugar
175 g (6 oz/½ cup) honey
2 large eggs, at room temperature
225 g (8 oz/1½ cups) plain (all-purpose) flour
1 teaspoon baking powder
1½ teaspoons ground cinnamon
½ teaspoon freshly grated nutmeg
½ teaspoon ground cardamom
a large pinch of ground cloves

SOFT MERINGUE TOPPING

145 g (5¼ oz/⅔ cup) caster (superfine) sugar
2 egg whites
¼ teaspoon cream of tartar

GOLDEN APRICOT DUMPLINGS WITH ORANGE POPPY SEED ICE CREAM

SERVES 6

ORANGE POPPY SEED ICE CREAM
100 g (3½ oz/⅔ cup) poppy seeds
125 ml (4 fl oz/½ cup) freshly squeezed orange
  juice, strained
310 ml (10¾ fl oz/1¼ cups) pouring (whipping)
  cream
310 ml (10¾ fl oz/1¼ cups) buttermilk
½ vanilla bean, split and scraped
3 large strips orange zest, white pith removed
½ teaspoon finely grated orange zest
9 large egg yolks
145 g (5¼ oz/⅔ cup) caster (superfine) sugar

APRICOT DUMPLINGS
12 good-quality dried apricots
3 tablespoons good-quality soft marzipan
  (almond paste)
plain (all-purpose) flour, for coating
2 eggs, lightly beaten
160 g (5½ oz/2 cups) fresh white breadcrumbs
sunflower oil, for deep-frying

APRICOT BRANDY SYRUP
80 g (2¾ oz/⅓ cup) caster (superfine) sugar
1 large strip orange zest, white pith removed
2 tablespoons freshly squeezed orange juice,
  strained
1½ tablespoons apricot brandy

To make the ice cream, grind the poppy seeds using a mortar and pestle, then put in a saucepan with the orange juice and bring to the boil over high heat. Cook for a few minutes, or until the orange juice has almost absorbed into the poppy seeds. Add the cream, buttermilk, vanilla bean and seeds and orange zest, and bring just to the boil again. Reduce the heat to a simmer and cook for 5 minutes, then remove from the heat and set aside to infuse for 15 minutes. Whisk the egg yolks and sugar in a bowl until smooth, then gradually whisk in the warm milk mixture. Pour into a clean saucepan and stir constantly over low–medium heat for about 10–12 minutes, or until the mixture coats the back of a spoon. Pour through a fine sieve into a bowl and cool slightly, then cover and refrigerate until well chilled. Churn in an ice-cream machine according to the manufacturer's instructions. Alternatively, you can transfer the mixture to a shallow metal tray and freeze, whisking every couple of hours until frozen and creamy. Freeze until ready to use.

To make the 'dumplings', put the apricots in a bowl and cover with boiling water. Set aside for 15–20 minutes, or until reconstituted. Drain well. Divide the marzipan into twelve even pieces and roll into balls; insert into the apricots through the hole where the seed was originally removed before they were dried. Lightly coat with plain flour, then dip into the egg and allow any excess to drip off. Roll in the breadcrumbs and refrigerate for 15 minutes to help the crumbs adhere.

To make the apricot brandy syrup, put the sugar, orange zest and 250 ml (9 fl oz/1 cup) water in a small saucepan over high heat and stir until the sugar has dissolved. Bring to a boil, then reduce the heat. Add the orange juice and brandy and simmer for 8 minutes, or until syrupy. Set aside to cool, then cover until ready to use. Discard the orange zest.

When you are ready to serve, fill a deep-fryer or large heavy-based saucepan one-third full of oil and heat to 180°C (350°F), or until a cube of bread dropped into the oil browns in 15 seconds. Fry the apricots, in batches, for 3–4 minutes each, or until golden. Drain on paper towels.

Serve the apricots hot with the syrup drizzled over and the ice cream on the side.

LIQUORICE CUSTARDS WITH COCONUT-LIME MACAROONS AND PLUMS

SERVES 8

Put the cream, milk and liquorice in a saucepan over a low–medium heat and slowly bring to a simmer. Cook for 8–10 minutes, or until the liquorice is just starting to disintegrate. Remove from the heat and allow to infuse for 15 minutes, then strain into a bowl, discarding the liquorice

Preheat the oven to 160°C (315°F/Gas 2–3). Whisk together the egg yolks, sugar, vanilla and liquorice root until smooth, then very gradually whisk in the warm cream mixture. Strain again and pour into eight 185 ml (6 fl oz/¾ cup) ramekins or other heatproof moulds.

Place the ramekins in a deep baking tray and fill with enough warm water to come 1 cm (½ inch) from the top of the ramekins. Cook for 50 minutes, or until just set and dry on top — the custards should still wobble a little. Carefully remove the ramekins from the water bath and cool for 30 minutes. Cover and refrigerate overnight.

To make the macaroons, preheat the oven to 120°C (235°F/Gas ½) and line baking trays with baking paper. Put the egg whites and the salt in a bowl and beat with electric beaters on high speed until soft peaks form. With the motor still running, gradually beat in the sugar until stiff peaks form. Fold in the lime zest and coconut. Working one at a time, drop 2 teaspoonfuls of mixture onto the prepared trays, making sure they are well spaced to allow for spreading. Flatten to about 1½ cm (⅝ inch) thick with a palette knife and repeat until all the mixture is used — you should make 24 macaroons in total. Cook for 15 minutes, or until dry to the touch. Turn off the oven and cool completely in the oven.

To serve, place some plums on each custard and serve with macaroons on the side.

Note: Macaroons can be stored in an airtight container for a couple of weeks and are typically served in Scandinavia and Germany during the Christmas season.

600 ml (21 fl oz) pouring (whipping) cream
300 ml (10½ fl oz) full-cream (whole) milk
6 soft liquorice sticks, chopped
10 large egg yolks
145 g (5¼ oz/⅔ cup) caster (superfine) sugar
½ teaspoon natural vanilla extract
¼ teaspoon finely grated liquorice root
24 small, good-quality preserved plums, to serve

COCONUT–LIME MACAROONS
2 egg whites, at room temperature
a pinch of salt
115 g (4 oz/½ cup) caster (superfine) sugar
½ teaspoon finely grated lime zest
60 g (2¼ oz/1 cup) shredded coconut, lightly toasted

PUMPKIN-SEED MARZIPAN PASTRIES WITH GLACE PUMPKIN

SERVES 6

500 g (1 lb 2 oz) butternut pumpkin (squash),
  top part only for a solid piece of seedless
  pumpkin
115 g (4 oz/½ cup) caster (superfine) sugar
625 ml (21½ fl oz/2½ cups) sweet German wine,
  preferably Spatzlese
½ vanilla bean, roughly chopped
1 tablespoon freshly squeezed lemon juice
buttermilk nutmeg ice cream (page 265) or
  ginger ice cream (page 216), to serve

PUMPKIN-SEED MARZIPAN PASTRIES

60 g (2¼ oz/½ cup) raw pepitas (green pumpkin
  seeds), plus 2 tablespoons, extra
80 g (2¾ oz/½ cup) blanched almonds
125 g (4½ oz/1 cup) icing (confectioners') sugar
1½ tablespoons plain (all-purpose) flour
2 tablespoons unsalted butter, softened
2 small eggs
1 tablespoon dark rum
6 sheets filo pastry
70 g (2½ oz) unsalted butter, melted

Cut the pumpkin into 2 cm (¾ inch) thick slices, then cut out 5 cm (2 inch) squares, making sure all the skin is removed from the edges — you need 6 pieces in total. Use a small sharp knife to bevel the edges of the squares, to help prevent them from breaking up during cooking.

Combine the sugar, wine, vanilla bean and lemon juice in a large, deep-sided frying pan over high heat. Add 125 ml (4 fl oz/½ cup) water and stir until the sugar has dissolved. Allow the mixture to come to the boil and cook for 5 minutes, then add the pumpkin pieces and when it comes to the boil again, reduce the heat and simmer for 20–25 minutes, or until the pumpkin is tender, but not breaking up. Remove from the heat and allow to cool completely in the syrup. When cooled, carefully remove the pumpkin with a slotted spoon and set aside on a tray. Strain the cooking liquid into a saucepan and return to high heat. Bring to the boil and cook for 5 minutes, or until thickened to a coating consistency. Remove from the heat and set aside to cool.

Meanwhile, make the pastries. Preheat the oven to 200°C (400°F/Gas 6). Finely grind the pepitas and almonds in a food processor, then add the icing sugar, flour, butter, eggs and rum, and process until as smooth as possible.

Lightly brush a filo sheet with melted butter. Place another sheet on top and brush with butter. Cut into two square-ish pieces, then fold each piece in half to form a long rectangle. Repeat with the remaining filo and butter to form six rectangles in total. Place a tablespoon of the pumpkin-seed marzipan at one end of each rectangle and spread out along the length of the short end, leaving a 1 cm (½ inch) border. Roll up the pastry, tucking in the sides to form a 'cigar' shape. Repeat with the remaining rectangles. Brush each with melted butter and sprinkle with the extra pepitas. Place on a baking tray and cook for 20 minutes, or until golden.

Place a piece of the glacé pumpkin on each serving plate and top with a pastry. Drizzle the syrup over the top and serve with a scoop of buttermilk nutmeg ice cream or ginger ice cream.

MOLTEN BLACK FOREST PUDDINGS WITH CHERRY COMPOTE AND KIRSCH CREAM

SERVES 6

Put the chocolate, cream and butter in a heatproof bowl and melt over a saucepan of simmering water, making sure the water does not touch the base of the bowl. Remove from the heat and cool slightly. Whisk together the eggs, sugar and flour until smooth. Add a couple of spoonfuls of the chocolate mixture and whisk in. Gradually mix in the rest of the chocolate with a rubber spatula until well combined. Cover and refrigerate until just firm enough to hold a fingerprint. Use a pastry brush to butter six 125 ml (4 fl oz/½ cup) dariole moulds. Sift the extra flour and cocoa together and lightly flour the moulds, tapping out any excess, then refrigerate until ready to use.

Meanwhile, make the cherry compote. Put the cherries, sugar and vanilla in a saucepan with 2 tablespoons water and bring to the boil over high heat. Reduce the heat and simmer for 15 minutes, or until the liquid has leached out of the cherries and is slightly syrupy. Stir in the cherry liqueur and kirsch and cook for 5 minutes, or until it becomes slightly syrupy again. Remove from the heat and leave to cool completely.

To make the kirsch cream, put the cream, icing sugar and kirsch in a chilled bowl and whip until fluffy. Cover and chill until ready to serve.

Preheat the oven to 200°C (400°F/Gas 6). Divide the chocolate mixture between the prepared moulds and place on a baking tray. Cook for 15 minutes, or until the top of each one is dry to the touch, slightly domed in the centre, and the puddings have shrunk away from the edges of the moulds. (It may take 1–2 minutes more or less, depending on your oven. For example, although your oven may read 200°C (400°F/Gas 6) it may in fact be 180°C (350°F/Gas 4) or 210°C (415°F/Gas 6–7), so I recommend an oven thermometer for dishes such as this, where precise temperature and timing is important.) For the best end result — a delicate crust and oozy chocolate centre — you need to catch the puddings at just the right moment, so keep an eye on them through the glass just before the 15-minute mark. Remove from the heat and allow to cool slightly in the moulds for 5 minutes, then carefully invert each of them onto a large plate or into a wide shallow bowl. Serve warm with the cherry compote and kirsch cream on the side.

200 g (7 oz) dark chocolate
75 ml (2⅔ fl oz) pouring (whipping) cream
40 g (1½ oz) unsalted butter
4 large eggs, at room temperature
115 g (4 oz/½ cup) caster (superfine) sugar
40 g (1½ oz/¼ cup) plain (all-purpose) flour, plus ½ tablespoon, extra
softened unsalted butter, for greasing
1 tablespoon unsweetened cocoa powder

CHERRY COMPOTE
300 g (10½ oz/1½ cups) frozen cherries
55 g (2 oz/¼ cup) caster (superfine) sugar
1 teaspoon natural vanilla extract
1½ tablespoons sweet dark cherry liqueur
1½ tablespoons kirsch or clear cherry schnapps

KIRSCH CREAM
185 ml (6 fl oz/¾ cup) pouring (whipping) cream
2½ tablespoons icing (confectioners') sugar, sifted
1½ tablespoons kirsch or clear cherry schnapps

PRUNE-FILLED CREPES BAKED IN CARAMEL WITH SPICED COOKIE CREAM

SERVES 6

CREPES
150 g (5½ oz/1 cup) plain (all-purpose) flour
a pinch of caster (superfine) sugar
a pinch of salt
3 eggs
185 ml (6 fl oz/¾ cup) full-cream (whole) milk
185 ml (6 fl oz/¾ cup) soda water
melted unsalted butter, for cooking

PRUNE FILLING
185 g (6½ oz/¾ cup) pitted prunes, chopped
½ vanilla bean, split
¼ teaspoon finely grated orange zest
2 tablespoons freshly squeezed orange juice, strained
2 tablespoons Slivovica (Polish plum brandy)

CARAMEL SAUCE
170 g (6 oz/¾ cup) caster (superfine) sugar
60 ml (2 fl oz/¼ cup) pouring (whipping) cream
1½ tablespoons Slivovica (Polish plum brandy)

SPICED COOKIE CREAM
4 x speculaas (pages 262–3) or use similar good-quality store-bought spiced cookies
50 g (1¾ oz/¼ cup) crème fraiche
2 tablespoons walnuts, toasted and chopped
125 ml (4 fl oz/½ cup) pouring (whipping) cream, whipped

To make the crepes, sift the flour, sugar and salt into a non-metallic bowl and make a well in the centre. Whisk together the eggs, milk, and soda water, pour into the well and whisk until smooth. Cover and set aside for 1 hour. Stir gently just prior to cooking.

Lightly brush a 23 cm (9 inch) crepe pan or non-stick frying pan with butter and place over medium heat. Pour 60 ml (2 fl oz/¼ cup) of the batter into the centre of the pan at a time, swirling to coat the base. Cook for 3–4 minutes, or until lightly golden, then turn and cook for a further 1 minute. Remove from the pan and repeat with the remaining crepe batter, brushing the pan occasionally with a little butter as needed. The first couple are usually inferior and can be discarded, so you should end up with 12 crepes in total. Cover and set aside until ready to use.

To make the prune filling, put the prunes, vanilla bean, orange zest and juice, Slivovica and 250 ml (9 fl oz/1 cup) water in a small saucepan and bring to the boil. Reduce the heat and simmer for 8 minutes, stirring regularly so the mixture doesn't stick to the pan, until the prunes are very soft. Remove from the heat and cool slightly, discarding the vanilla bean.

To make the caramel sauce, put the sugar and 125 ml (4 fl oz/½ cup) water in a saucepan and stir over high heat until the sugar has dissolved. Bring to the boil and cook for 10 minutes, without stirring, or until golden. Quickly but carefully, as it will spit, whisk in the cream and then the Slivovica, and cook for 2-3 minutes, or until thickened. Remove from the heat.

Meanwhile, crush the cookies and mix with the crème fraiche, and walnuts, then fold in the whipped cream. Cover and refrigerate until ready to use.

Preheat the oven to 180°C (350°F/Gas 4). Spread the prune filling thinly over the crepes with the back of a spoon that has been dipped in hot water, then fold the crepes in half, then in half again to form a wedge shape. Lightly grease a 22 cm (8½ inch) round baking dish and lay the crepes in the base, overlapping slightly. Pour the caramel sauce over the top and bake for 10 minutes, or until bubbling.

Serve the crepes with a dollop of the cookie cream, and a small glass of Slivovica, of course!

DREAMING OF A WHITE CHRISTMAS

FEW MOMENTS IN LIFE EVOKE THE ENCHANTMENT OF A SNOW-CLOAKED CHRISTMAS. SPICE AND PINE-SCENTED ROOMS DECKED IN COLOURS OF JOY SUPPORT A MAGICAL BLEND OF TRADITION, FOLKLORE AND INDULGENT FEASTING. WHEN THIS SPECIAL DAY IS ICED IN GLISTENING WHITE IT'S GUARANTEED TO MELT THE HEARTS OF EVEN THE COOLEST CHARACTERS AND MAKE FOR A MEMORABLE CELEBRATION.

GINGERBREAD SPICE GLAZED HAM WITH CHERRY RELISH

SERVES UP TO 20 AS PART OF A BUFFET

Preheat the oven to 180°C (350°F/Gas 4). Using a very sharp knife, cut a straight line through the skin around the shank of the ham, 7 cm (2¾ inches) in from the end. Carefully insert your thumb under the cut edge which faces away from the shank to make an air pocket between the skin and the fat. Start to pull the skin away from the fat in the direction of the large end of the ham, away from the shank. Continue this process, easing the skin away by running one hand under it and pulling the skin away with the other hand until the skin comes off in one large piece.

Lightly score the fat to form a diamond pattern. Be careful not to score too deeply because if you cut through to the meat, the fat will fall off during cooking. Combine all the remaining ingredients, except the cloves, and mix until smooth. Place a clove in the centre of each diamond, then spread half the glaze over the ham avoiding the shank.

Place the ham on a sturdy rack in a large roasting tin and pour 500 ml (17 fl oz/2 cups) water into the base of the tin. Lightly cover the ham with foil, firmly securing the foil to the edges of the tin. Cook for 50 minutes, then remove from the oven and increase the oven temperature to 210°C (415°F/Gas 6–7). Remove the foil, brush over the remaining glaze, being careful to avoid knocking off any cloves and return to the oven, uncovered. Cook for a further 25 minutes, or until the surface of the ham is caramelised. Remove from the oven and set aside to rest for at least 15 minutes before carving.

While the ham is cooking, make the cherry relish. Place all the ingredients in a saucepan with a large pinch of salt and stir over high heat until the sugar has dissolved. Allow to just come to the boil, then reduce the heat and simmer for 40–45 minutes, or until most of the liquid has been absorbed. The small amount of liquid that is left will thicken on cooling, making the relish more glazy. Serve warm or at room temperature with the ham.

7 kg (15 lb 12 oz) smoked, cooked leg ham
125 g (4½ oz/⅔ cup) soft brown sugar
4 tablespoons golden syrup or dark corn syrup
1 tablespoon sweet Bavarian or German mustard
2 tablespoons freshly squeezed orange juice, strained
1½ teaspoons ground ginger
½ teaspoon ground cinnamon
¼ teaspoon ground nutmeg
¼ teaspoon ground allspice
whole cloves, for decorating

CHERRY RELISH

600 g (1 lb 5 oz/3 cups) frozen cherries, defrosted
1½ tablespoons soft brown sugar
1 tablespoon yellow or brown mustard seeds
1 garlic clove, very finely chopped
½ small red onion, very finely chopped
½ teaspoon ground cinnamon
2½ tablespoons cider vinegar
½ teaspoon finely chopped orange zest
2 tablespoons freshly squeezed orange juice, strained

ROLLED PISTACHIO STUFFED PORK LOIN WITH CARROT AND MOLASSES BAKE

SERVES 10–12

2.2 kg (4 lb 15 oz) pork loin roast, ask your
  butcher to butterfly it and score the skin
100 g (3½ oz) minced (ground) pork
100 g (3½ oz) minced (ground) veal
160 g (5½ oz/2 cups) fresh white breadcrumbs
1 egg
60 g (2¼ oz/¼ cup) sour cream
50 g (1¾ oz/⅓ cup) peeled pistachios
½ teaspoon ground cardamom
1 teaspoon ground coriander
1½ teaspoons freshly grated nutmeg
1 teaspoon ground ginger
½ teaspoon white pepper
3 garlic cloves, crushed
½ teaspoon dried marjoram
1 large handful of flat-leaf (Italian) parsley,
  finely chopped
3 large brown onions, thickly sliced
1 tablespoon olive oil
sea salt, to taste

CARROT AND MOLASSES BAKE
1.5 kg (3 lb 5 oz) carrots, peeled and chopped
2 tablespoons butter
1½ tablespoons molasses
½ teaspoon ground ginger
¼ teaspoon freshly grated nutmeg
125 ml (4 fl oz/½ cup) pouring (whipping)
  cream
3 eggs, separated
1½ teaspoons fine sea salt
¼ teaspoon white pepper

Preheat the oven to 200°C (400°F/Gas 6). Lay the pork, skin side down, on a clean work surface. Put all the remaining ingredients, except for the onion, olive oil and sea salt, in a bowl and combine thoroughly with very clean hands, mixing together to ensure the spices go right through. Season with a little salt. Pat the mixture into a log shape, about 6 cm (2½ inches) thick and 18 cm (7 inches) long, position down the centre of the pork loin and roll up the pork. Use kitchen string to tie the loin together so it holds its shape during cooking.

Make a bed of sliced onion in the base of a roasting tin and sit the pork loin on top. Pour 250 ml (9 fl oz/1 cup) water into the base of the tin. Rub the pork all over with the olive oil and liberally sprinkle with sea salt. Cook in the oven for 1 hour 50 minutes to 2 hours, or until the crackling is crisp and golden all over and a skewer comes out hot when inserted directly through the stuffing (not through the meat) — it is very important that the stuffing is thoroughly cooked through. Remove from the oven, cover, and rest for 20 minutes before carving.

Meanwhile, cook the carrots in boiling water for 30 minutes, or until very tender. Drain, cool slightly and purée in a food processor or blender until very smooth. Add the butter, molasses, ginger, nutmeg, cream, egg yolks, sea salt and white pepper and process again to combine well. Cool to room temperature. Whisk the egg whites until medium peaks form then fold into the carrot mixture. Carefully pour into a lightly greased deep baking dish and add to the oven about 30 minutes before the pork has finished cooking. The carrot and molasses bake should be cooked until puffed and golden.

Carve the pork and serve with the carrot and molasses bake and perhaps some cranberry sauce or lingonberry preserves on the side.

ROAST TURKEY WITH CHESTNUT STUFFING AND VIN SANTO GRAPE SAUCE

SERVES UP TO 20 AS PART OF A CHRISTMAS BUFFET, 12 AS A MAIN COURSE

CHESTNUT STUFFING

300 g (10½ oz/2 cups) fresh chestnuts

55 g (2 oz/⅓ cup) raisins, chopped

2 tablespoons Vin Santo or Sauternes

3 tablespoons butter

1 large brown onion, finely chopped

150 g (5½ oz) piece pancetta, finely diced

80 g (2¾ oz/½ cup) lightly toasted pine nuts

1 rosemary sprig, leaves finely chopped

2 teaspoons chopped thyme leaves

1 large handful flat-leaf (Italian) parsley, finely chopped

½ teaspoon finely grated lemon zest

1 teaspoon freshly grated nutmeg

4 thick slices day-old white bread, crusts removed and cut into small dice

170 ml (5½ fl oz/⅔ cup) full-cream (whole) milk

Preheat the oven to 200°C (400°F/Gas 6). To make the stuffing, use the point of a small knife to cut a small slit in the rounded stem end of each chestnut. Put them into a large saucepan, cover with cold water and bring to the boil over high heat. Cook for 15 minutes, then drain. Cool slightly, then peel and roughly chop the flesh. Set aside in a large bowl.

Place the raisins and Vin Santo in a small saucepan with 2 tablespoons water and bring to the boil. Reduce the heat and simmer for about 5 minutes, or until the liquid is almost evaporated. Set aside.

Melt the butter in a frying pan over medium–high heat and add the onion and pancetta. Cook for 10–12 minutes, or until the onion is golden. Place the mixture in the bowl with the chestnuts and add the raisins, pine nuts, herbs, lemon zest, nutmeg, bread and milk. Combine well, then set aside for 10 minutes, or until the bread has absorbed the milk. Season to taste.

Remove any giblets and neck from the turkey and place in the bottom of a large roasting tin with the onion, carrot and celery. Rinse the bird, inside and out, and pat dry with paper towels or a very clean tea towel (dish towel). Thoroughly combine the butter, garlic, thyme and 1 teaspoon of the sea salt. Carefully slide a very clean hand between the turkey breast and the skin to loosen enough to add the garlic butter. Be careful not to tear. Use your fingers to place the butter under the skin and spread evenly over the breast meat, patting the skin back down. Spoon the stuffing inside the cavity, ensuring it is fairly loosely packed.

Place a large sturdy wire rack in the tin over the vegetables and sit the bird on top. Tuck the wings under the body and tie the legs together to help keep the natural shape of the bird. Rub all over with olive oil and season with the remaining sea salt. Pour the stock and 375 ml (13 fl oz/ 1½ cups) water into the base of the roasting tin. Cover the turkey loosely with long sheets of foil, sealing tightly around the edges of the tin. Cook in the oven for 1 hour, lifting the foil to baste with the pan juices after 30 minutes. Reduce the temperature to 190°C (375°F/Gas 5) and cook for a further 2 hours, basting the turkey every 30 minutes or so and turning the tin occasionally to ensure even cooking. Remove the foil and cook for 1 hour further, or until golden all over and the juices run clear when you insert a skewer into the thickest part of the thigh.

Remove the turkey from the oven, carefully transfer to a large warmed serving platter and cover with foil to keep warm; let it rest for 25–30 minutes. Strain the juices from the roasting tin into a large bowl with a lip and allow to settle, discarding the turkey giblets, neck and vegetables. Spoon 80 ml (2½ fl oz/⅓ cup) of the fat from the bowl and place back in the roasting tin. Sit the tin on two stove burners over medium–high heat. Scatter over the flour and cook for 2–3 minutes, scraping up any cooked-on bits with a wooden spoon. Use a balloon whisk to gradually stir in the Vin Santo, the juices from the bowl and any juices that accumulate from the resting turkey, until you have a smooth gravy. Add a little extra chicken stock or water if needed. Add the grapes and cook for a further 3 minutes, or until warmed through; season to taste.

Carve the turkey and serve with the stuffing and gravy.

7.5 kg (16 lb 14 oz) turkey
1 brown onion, chopped
2 carrots, diced
2 celery stalks, diced
80 g (2¾ oz) butter, softened
4 garlic cloves, crushed
2 teaspoons finely chopped thyme
3 teaspoons sea salt
olive oil, for rubbing over
1 litre (35 fl oz/4 cups) chicken stock
3 tablespoons plain (all-purpose) flour
125 ml (4 fl oz/½ cup) Vin Santo or Sauternes
270 g (9½ oz/1½ cups) seedless green grapes, halved

ROAST GOOSE WITH APPLE, CIDER VINEGAR GRAVY AND GOLDEN POTATOES

SERVES 6

1.5 kg (3 lb 5 oz) all-purpose potatoes, such as desiree, unpeeled and washed well

3 kg (6 lb 12 oz) goose (if frozen, make sure it is completely defrosted)

1 large brown onion, finely chopped

1 large celery stalk, finely chopped

5 bay leaves, crushed, plus extra, to garnish

2 teaspoons allspice berries

1 cinnamon stick, halved

fine sea salt

500 ml (17 fl oz/2 cups) chicken stock

4 apples

2 tablespoons plain (all-purpose) flour

60 ml (2 fl oz/¼ cup) cider vinegar

60 ml (2 fl oz/¼ cup) apple juice

Preheat the oven to 210°C (415°F/Gas 6–7). Cook the potatoes in boiling water for 20 minutes, or until just starting to become tender. Drain well, cool and then peel and cut in half or into large chunks and set aside until ready to roast.

Remove any innards from the goose and discard. Rub the cavity with salt, then rinse inside and out and pat dry with paper towels or a very clean tea towel (dish towel). Put the combined onion, celery, two of the bay leaves, allspice berries and cinnamon stick inside the cavity. Take a fine skewer and carefully prick the skin all over, ensuring you don't pierce the flesh — the best way to do this is to hold the skewer almost horizontally against the goose and insert sideways.

Rub the goose all over with fine sea salt and place, breast side up, on a sturdy 'v' rack in a large roasting tin. Roast in the oven for 30 minutes, or until the skin is just starting to change colour, then baste with any accumulated goose fat. Remove the goose from the oven, reduce the temperature to 140°C (275°F/Gas 1) then cook the goose a further 1 hour 45 minutes. Spoon off all the fat into a bowl and set aside. Pour the chicken stock into the base of the tin, loosely cover the bird with a few long pieces of foil, securing the foil against the edge of the tin to help hold its place. Cook for a further 1 hour 30 minutes, basting regularly with some of the reserved goose fat, then remove the foil, increase the heat to 200°C (400°F/Gas 6) and continue to cook for 30 minutes, or until the juices run clear when the thickest part of the thigh is pierced with a skewer and the bird is deep golden and crispy all over. Remove from the oven, carefully transfer the goose to a warmed serving platter and cover with foil to keep warm while it rests for about 25 minutes. Tip any juices from the roasting tin into a bowl and set aside.

In the last half hour of the goose cooking time, pour about 250 ml (9 fl oz/1 cup) of the reserved goose fat into the base of a second large roasting tin, add the remaining bay leaves and heat in the oven until hot. Add the potatoes and carefully toss to coat in the fat. Cook for 45 minutes, or until the goose has rested and been carved — the potatoes should be golden and crisp. Use a slotted spoon to remove the potatoes from the fat and season to taste with sea salt. Place in a warmed serving dish.

While the potatoes are cooking, prepare the apples. Don't peel the apples but core them and wash well; cut into 1½ cm (⅝ inch) thick rings. Heat 2 tablespoons of the remaining goose fat in a large frying pan over medium–high heat and cook the apple slices, in batches, for 2 minutes on each side, or until golden and tender. Carefully tip off any juices accumulating under the resting goose plus any from its cavity into the bowl you have set aside with the juices from the roasting tin. While it sits the fat will rise to the top — you will need this shortly. Arrange the apple slices and extra bay leaves around the edge of the turkey on the serving platter. Re-cover and keep warm.

Remove all of the fat from the top of the reserved cooking juices and place 3 tablespoons of the fat in the roasting tin, discarding the rest. Place the tin over two stove burners on medium–high. Sprinkle with the flour and use a whisk to mix the flour into the fat and cook for 1 minute. Gradually whisk in the vinegar and apple juice and mix until smooth, then gradually add the reserved cooking juices from the goose, whisking continuously, until you have a smooth thin sauce. Allow to bubble away, still whisking, for about 5 minutes, or until the sauce thickens to a light coating consistency; season to taste.

Serve the goose and apples at the table for carving, with the potatoes and the gravy on the side. This also goes well with spiced red cabbage (page 131) and some greens, such as brussels sprouts or beans.

WHOLE ROAST SALMON WITH SKAGEN BUTTER, CARDAMOM CARAMEL POTATOES AND CREAMED PEAS

SERVES 10–12

SKAGEN (PRAWN, CAVIAR AND RED ONION) BUTTER

250 g (9 oz) butter, softened

2½ tablespoons small orange roe, preferably flying fish roe

6 cooked king prawns, peeled, deveined and finely chopped

½ small red onion, very finely diced

½ teaspoon finely chopped lemon zest

1 small handful dill, finely chopped

white pepper, to taste

CARDAMOM CARAMEL POTATOES

2 kg (4 lb 8 oz) new potatoes (chats), peeled

115 g (4 oz/½ cup) caster (superfine) sugar

125 g (4½ oz) butter

a large pinch of ground cardamom

CREAMED PEAS

500 g (1 lb 2 oz) frozen peas

2 tablespoons butter

125 g (4½ oz/½ cup) sour cream

white pepper, to taste

To make the skagen butter, combine all the ingredients in a bowl, stirring well. Season with plenty of salt and white pepper. Spoon in a log shape onto some plastic wrap, then roll up, twisting the ends of the plastic to make a firm sausage shape. Refrigerate until ready to serve.

Preheat the oven to 190°C (375°F/Gas 5). Cook the potatoes in salted boiling water for 15 minutes, or until tender. Drain well, cover to keep warm, and set aside.

To make the creamed peas, cook the peas in boiling water for about 5 minutes, or until tender, then drain well. Combine the peas with the butter and sour cream in a food processor and blend until smooth. Tip into a small saucepan and season to taste with salt and a little white pepper. Cover and set side until ready to serve.

Rinse the salmon inside and out and pat dry with paper towels or a very clean tea towel (dish towel). Insert half the onion, lemon slices and dill sprigs in the cavity. Rub all over with a little olive oil and sprinkle with sea salt. Wrap the head and tail with foil. Make a bed of the remaining onion and lemon in the base of the tin and lay a long piece of muslin (cheesecloth) over the top, making sure it hangs a little over the two short edges — this will act as handles for removing the fish later on. Place the fish on top of the cloth. Pour the wine and 250 ml (9 fl oz/1 cup) of water into the base of the tin. Cook the fish in the oven for about 45 minutes, basting regularly with the juices, until the dorsel fin is very loose or comes off when jiggled. At this stage the fish should be cooked through but still quite pink and translucent in the centre of the fillet.

Meanwhile, to caramelise the potatoes, place the sugar in a large heavy-based frying pan over medium–high heat, stirring occasionally until the sugar has melted. Bring to the boil, then reduce the heat and simmer for 5 minutes, or until it turns golden. Carefully stir in the butter and cardamom — the caramel will become lumpy but will melt as you continue to cook. Add the potatoes and shake the pan for 6 minutes, or until the potatoes are caramelised and heated through. Season to taste and keep warm.

Gently reheat the creamed peas, if necessary. Lift the salmon out of the roasting tin using the muslin to help you. Carefully transfer onto a warmed serving platter, gently sliding the cloth from under it. If you find it difficult to remove the cloth, simply use some sharp scissors to cut around the edges close to the fish. Remove the foil from the head and tail. Carefully peel back the skin from the top side of the fish, starting at the head end and pulling towards the tail; discard the skin.

Serve portions of the fish on a bed of the creamed peas with a dollop of the skagen butter on top and the potatoes on the side.

3.5 kg (7 lb 14 oz) whole, cleaned and scaled salmon
2 red onions, thinly sliced
2 lemons, thinly sliced
3 large dill sprigs
olive oil, for coating
sea salt
125 ml (4 fl oz/½ cup) dry white wine

HERB-STUFFED ROLLED VEAL BREAST BAKED IN CREAM

SERVES 8

Preheat the oven to 210°C (415°F/Gas 6–7). To make the stuffing, tear the bread into small pieces and soak in the milk for 10 minutes, or until most of the milk has been absorbed. Squeeze out any excess milk and combine the bread with the remaining stuffing ingredients. Season well with salt and white pepper.

Combine the mustard and garlic. Lay the veal on your work surface with the meat from the ribs facing up and the thickest end closest to you. Using a meat mallet, carefully bash the meat out to a thickness of about 2 cm (¾ inch). Spread the stuffing mixture evenly over the breast and carefully roll the breast away from you to form a log. Place a large piece of baking paper on the work surface in front of you with the short ends left to right. Lay the bacon slices on top of the paper, slightly overlapping, to form a blanket of bacon in front of you. Carefully place the rolled veal along the edge of the bacon closest to you. Spread half of the mustard mixture over the exposed part of the veal. Carefully roll the veal away from you, exposing the underside, and spread with the remaining mustard mixture. Carefully roll the veal up with the bacon, using the baking paper to help. Tie around the veal with kitchen string at regular intervals to secure the bacon.

Put the onion and bay leaves in the base of a large 50 x 30 cm (20 x 12 inch) baking dish. Sit the veal on top — you may need to curve the veal slightly to fit. Pour over the combined Riesling, stock, cream and lemon juice. Bake for 10 minutes, or until the bacon is starting to brown, then reduce the temperature to 170°C (325°F/Gas 3) and cook, spooning over the marinade mixture every 15 minutes for a further 2½ hours, or until the veal is cooked through and tender. Remove from the oven, cover the tin with foil and rest for 15 minutes, then remove the veal to a serving platter and cover to keep warm while reducing the sauce.

Place the tin over two stove burners and bring to the boil. Cook for 15 minutes, or until thickened to a coating consistency. Slice the veal into 3 cm (1¼ inch) thick slices and serve with the sauce spooned over the top. Serve with boiled potatoes tossed with tarragon and butter, bread dumplings (pages 112–13) or mashed potatoes and lightly cooked green vegetables.

STUFFING

8 slices white bread, crusts removed
125 ml (4 fl oz/½ cup) full-cream (whole) milk
1 small onion, grated and squeezed to extract excess liquid
2 teaspoons finely chopped tarragon
1 large handful flat-leaf (Italian) parsley, finely chopped
2 teaspoons capers, rinsed, drained and finely chopped
½ teaspoon freshly grated nutmeg
1 egg
white pepper, to season

3 tablespoons mild Austrian mustard
2 garlic cloves, crushed
2 kg (4 lb 8 oz) boned veal breast in one piece, ask your butcher to remove any excess sinew
12 long bacon slices, rind removed
1 large brown onion, very finely sliced
2 bay leaves
125 ml (4 fl oz/½ cup) Riesling
500 ml (17 fl oz/2 cups) good-quality veal stock
500 ml (17 fl oz/2 cups) pouring (whipping) cream
1 tablespoon freshly squeezed lemon juice

CARAWAY ROAST PORK RACK, PEAR SAUCE AND MUSTARD ONION MASH

SERVES 8

3 teaspoons caraway seeds

2 teaspoons fennel seeds

½ teaspoon dried marjoram

1 teaspoon freshly ground black pepper

2.5 kg (5 lb 8 oz) rack of pork, ask your butcher to score the skin

1 large brown onion, chopped

1 carrot, chopped

2 celery stalks, chopped

250 ml (9 fl oz/1 cup) wheat or pale ale beer

1½ tablespoons sea salt

3 tablespoons plain (all-purpose) flour

375 ml (13 fl oz/1½ cups) chicken stock

PEAR SAUCE

3 ripe pears, peeled, cored and diced

1 tablespoon soft brown sugar

½ teaspoon finely grated lemon zest

Coarsely grind the caraway and fennel seeds using a mortar and pestle or in a spice grinder then combine with the marjoram and pepper. Rub the spices all over the pork rack and make sure to push the mixture into the scored skin. Cover and refrigerate overnight.

Preheat the oven to 200°C (400°F/Gas 6). Put the chopped onion, carrot, celery, beer and 375 ml (13 fl oz/1½ cups) water in the base of a large roasting tin. Put a roasting rack in the tin, sit the pork on top and rub the sea salt evenly over the scored skin. Place on the lowest shelf of the oven and cook for 1½ hours, or until the crackling is very crisp and golden and the meat gives just a little resistance when you press it firmly at both ends. Cover loosely with foil if the crackling browns before the meat is cooked.

While the pork is cooking, make the pear sauce. Place all of the ingredients in a saucepan with 80 ml (2½ fl oz/⅓ cup) water and bring to the boil over high heat. Reduce the heat and simmer for 12–15 minutes, or until the pear is very tender. Remove from the heat, purée in a blender, and season to taste. Return the sauce to a clean saucepan and set aside to be reheated when ready to serve.

To make the mustard onion mash, heat one-third of the butter with the olive oil in a frying pan over medium–high heat. Add the sliced onion and sea salt and cook for 5 minutes, stirring occasionally. Add the mustard seeds and cook for a further 10 minutes, or until the onion is golden and slightly crisp on the edges.

Meanwhile, cook the potatoes in boiling water for 15 minutes, or until very tender. Drain well, then add the remaining butter, garlic and sour cream and mash until smooth. Stir through the onion mixture and season to taste. Cover and keep warm until ready to serve.

When the pork is cooked, remove from the oven and transfer to a warmed serving platter. Cover with foil to keep warm and rest for 15–20 minutes before serving.

While the pork rests, tip off any juices from the roasting tin, discarding the vegetables. Allow the juices to settle, then spoon off the fat, reserving 3 tablespoons for the gravy. Put the roasting tin over two stove burners on high. Add the reserved fat, sprinkle over the flour and stir, scraping up any cooked-on bits. Gradually whisk in the reserved roasting juices and the stock until you have a smooth, thin sauce. Allow to bubble away for a few minutes, or until thickened slightly, stirring in any resting juices which will now have accumulated in the serving dish. Strain the gravy and season to taste.

Gently reheat the pear sauce and mustard onion mash, if necessary. Carve the pork and serve with the mash, gravy and pear sauce. For extra sides, add some fried slices of blood sausage, bought sauerkraut or pickled cabbage (page 109), or bread dumplings (page 112–3).

MUSTARD ONION MASH
125 g (4½ oz) butter
2 tablespoons olive oil
2 large brown onions, thinly sliced
1 teaspoon sea salt
3 teaspoons brown mustard seeds
2 kg (4 lb 8 oz) all-purpose potatoes, such as desiree, peeled and diced
1 garlic clove, crushed
375 g (13 oz/1½ cups) sour cream

PHEASANT IN PLUM BRANDY WITH POTATO AND CABBAGE PANCAKES AND PRUNE SAUCE

SERVES 6

3 x 1 kg (2 lb 4 oz) pheasants, innards
  discarded, necks retained
125 ml (4 fl oz/½ cup) Slivovica (Polish plum
  brandy)
1 brown onion, finely chopped
1 large carrot, very finely diced
1 large celery stalk, very finely diced
4 bay leaves, crushed
3 garlic cloves, bruised
1½ teaspoons juniper berries, lightly crushed
1 teaspoon ground cinnamon
1 teaspoon ground ginger
125 ml (4 fl oz/½ cup) freshly squeezed orange
  juice, strained
2 bacon slices, finely chopped, plus 3 slices
  extra (streaky part only), halved
125 g (4½ oz) butter, softened

Rinse the pheasants well inside and out and pat dry with paper towels or a very clean tea towel (dish towel). Place in a large non-metallic bowl. Combine the Slivovica, onion, carrot, celery, bay leaves, garlic cloves, juniper berries, cinnamon, ginger, orange juice and chopped bacon and pour over the pheasants, turning the pheasants to coat and spooning some of the marinade into the cavities of each bird. Cover with plastic wrap and marinate in the fridge for 48 hours, turning occasionally.

On the day you are to serve, prepare the potato and cabbage pancakes. Mix all the ingredients together except the oil and seasoned flour, and season well. Divide the mixture into six even-sized patties with an 8 cm (3¼ inch) diameter and about 1 cm (½ inch) thick. Place in a single layer on a baking tray, cover, and refrigerate until ready to cook.

Preheat the oven to 200°C (400°F/Gas 6). Take the birds out of the marinade, reserving the marinade for the sauce. Carefully loosen the skin over the breasts and use your fingers to smear some butter over each breast, under the skin, then neatly pull the skin back over. Smear any remaining butter over the top of the birds and season with salt and a little freshly ground black pepper. Tie the legs together to help hold the birds' shape, then lay two pieces of streaky bacon lengthways over the breast of each bird. Place a wire rack in a roasting tin and place the birds, breast side up, on the rack. Pour 625 ml (21½ fl oz/2½ cups) water into the base of the tin and cook for 15 minutes. Decrease the heat to 180°C (350°F/Gas 4) and remove the bacon. Cook the pheasants for 55 minutes, basting regularly with the pan juices, until golden and the juices run clear when a skewer is inserted into the thickest part of the thigh. Remove from the oven, cover with foil and keep warm for 10–15 minutes to rest before serving.

While the pheasants are cooking, make the prune sauce. Put the marinade ingredients in a large saucepan with the stock, orange zest and 125 ml (4 fl oz/½ cup) water. Bring to the boil over high heat and cook for 15 minutes, or until the liquid is reduced to about 250 ml (9 fl oz/1 cup), then strain into a clean saucepan and add the prunes. Return to the boil, then reduce the heat and simmer for 10 minutes, or until there is only about 170 ml (5½ fl oz/⅔ cup) of liquid left. Cover and set aside.

To cook the potato and cabbage pancakes, pour enough oil into a large frying pan to come 1 cm (½ inch) up the side of the pan and heat over medium–high heat. When the oil is hot, lightly coat the pancakes in the seasoned flour and cook, in batches, for 2–3 minutes on each side, or until golden and heated through. Season to taste.

When the birds are rested, tip the resting juices into the prune sauce and reheat the sauce.

Cut the pheasants in half and serve with the pancakes and the prune sauce on the side for spooning over. Serve with some lightly cooked greens.

POTATO AND CABBAGE CAKES
900 g (2 lb/4 cups) plain mashed potato
75 g (2½ oz/½ cup) self-raising flour
75 g (2⅔ oz/1 cup) shredded cabbage
1 handful chives, finely snipped
60 g (2¼ oz/¼ cup) sour cream
1 egg
sunflower oil, for pan-frying
seasoned plain (all-purpose) flour, for coating

PRUNE SAUCE
500 ml (17 fl oz/2 cups) good-quality veal stock
½ teaspoon finely grated orange zest
12 pitted prunes, halved

BIGOS HUNTERS STEW

SERVES 10–12

Place the duck legs, skin side down, in the base of a large saucepan or stockpot and place over medium heat. Cook for 7 minutes, or until dark golden, then remove the duck to a plate. Remove all but 3 tablespoons of duck fat from the pan. Add the onions and cook for 15 minutes, stirring occasionally, until golden. Add the garlic and stir for 30 seconds, or until fragrant. Return the duck to the pan along with the remaining ingredients and add 1 litre (35 fl oz/4 cups) water. Bring to the boil over high heat, then reduce the heat and simmer for 2½ hours, stirring occasionally, until all the meats are very tender. Remove from the heat and allow to sit for 45 minutes, or until cool enough to transfer the pan to the fridge. Cover and refrigerate for 24–48 hours to allow the flavours to develop.

When ready to serve, remove the stew from the refrigerator and skim off any fat from the surface. Place the pan over medium–high heat and bring just to the boil. Reduce the heat and simmer for 10 minutes, or until heated through. Remove the ham hock and duck to a chopping board. Slice the hock into 5 cm (2 inch) pieces. Cut the duck legs in half through the joint. Return the hock and duck pieces to the pan and stir through. Season to taste and serve the bigos immediately with potatoes and sour cream or dark rye bread with butter and some green vegetables on the side. Meats can be cut into smaller portions depending on the number of guests and dishes, or courses, you are serving.

Variation: For something a little different, try adding rabbit, wild boar, beef or lamb.

Note: If fresh porcini (cep) mushrooms are in season, you can substitute 150 g (5½ oz) of fresh for the dried mushroom.

5 x 220 g (7¾ oz) duck leg quarters, skin pricked all over
2 large brown onions, chopped
3 garlic cloves, chopped
1 kg (2 lb 4 oz) sauerkraut, rinsed and drained
500 g (1 lb 2 oz) good-quality kielbasa (Polish sausage)
800 g (1 lb 12 oz) smoked ham hock
400 g (14 oz) boneless pork belly, cut into 5 cm (2 inch) cubes
500 g (1 lb 2 oz) venison shin meat, cut into 5 cm (2 inch) cubes
1.5 litres (52 fl oz/6 cups) beef stock
750 ml (26 fl oz/3 cups) red wine
8 pitted prunes, chopped
2 apples, peeled and grated
2 tablespoons dried porcini (cep) mushrooms
10 juniper berries
2 bay leaves
1 teaspoon caraway seeds

TRUFFLED CHICKEN BREASTS WITH LEEKS AND A CHAMPAGNE CREAM SAUCE

SERVES 6

3 leeks, white part only
60 g (2¼ oz) butter, softened
500 ml (17 fl oz/2 cups) chicken stock
6 organic chicken supreme (breast fillet with
  wing attached), skin on
1 small black truffle (about 20 g/¾ oz),
  preferably fresh
fine sea salt, to season
1 tablespoon olive oil

CHAMPAGNE CREAM SAUCE

2 teaspoons butter
1 garlic clove, crushed
1 tablespoon plain (all-purpose) flour
80 ml (2½ fl oz/⅓ cup) Champagne
125 ml (4 fl oz/½ cup) pouring (whipping)
  cream
125 ml (4 fl oz/½ cup) chicken stock
1 thyme sprig
sea salt, to taste
white pepper, to taste
black truffle oil (optional)

Preheat the oven to 190°C (375°F/Gas 5). Cut each leek into two even lengths, then cut each piece in half lengthways so you have 12 pieces. Place a single layer of leek, cut side up, in a roasting tin that just fits them snugly. Dot 40 g (1½ oz) of the butter over the top and pour over the stock. Season with salt and freshly ground black pepper and cook in the oven for 30 minutes, or until just starting to become tender.

Meanwhile, carefully loosen the skin on the chicken breasts. Very finely slice or shave the truffle and insert a few pieces, one by one, under the skin of each breast, being very careful not to tear the skin. Smooth the skin back over and season with sea salt. If you like, you can use a toothpick to attach the edge of the skin to the pointy end of the breast so the skin doesn't shrink when cooking, but take them out before serving!

Heat the remaining butter and the oil in a large heavy-based frying pan over medium–high heat and add the chicken breasts, skin side down. Cook for 3 minutes on each side, or until lightly golden. Remove the chicken to a plate and reserve the pan with the cooking juices for making the sauce.

When the leeks are just tender, remove from the oven and place the breasts over the top of the leek, skin side up. Return to the oven and cook for about 15 minutes, or until the chicken breasts are just cooked through and the skin is a deep golden and crispy. Remove the breasts and leeks from the oven. Place the breasts on a lightly warmed tray and cover to keep warm while they rest for 5 minutes. Drain off 80 ml (2½ fl oz/⅓ cup) cooking liquid from the leeks and reserve for the sauce. Cover the leeks with foil and set aside.

While the chicken is resting, make the sauce. Heat the butter in the reserved frying pan over medium–high heat. Add the garlic and stir for a few seconds, or until fragrant. Sprinkle over the flour and stir, scraping up any cooked-on bits from the bottom of the pan. Using a balloon whisk, gradually mix in the combined Champagne, cream, reserved cooking liquid from the leeks and stock, until you have a smooth thin liquid. Add the thyme and bring to the boil. Reduce the heat and simmer for 3 minutes, stirring regularly, until thickened to a coating consistency. Stir in any resting juices from the chicken breasts. Season to taste with sea salt and a little white pepper, then add a few drops of truffle oil, if desired (if the truffle in the chicken breast is fresh and good-quality you should not need the truffle oil).

Transfer the leeks to a warmed serving platter in a neat row and place the chicken breasts on top. Serve with the sauce on the side for each guest to spoon over.

This dish is lovely served with some lightly cooked asparagus and sautéed wild mushrooms, if available. Potatoes, either crisp and crunchy or smoothly mashed are also ideal.

DANISH RICE PUDDING WITH CHERRY SAUCE

SERVES 6

Put the vanilla bean and seeds, milk, cream, cinnamon, cardamom and lemon zest in a large saucepan over high heat and bring just to the boil. Stir in the rice, then when it returns to the boil, reduce the heat and simmer for 30 minutes, stirring regularly. Add the sugar and stir until dissolved. Continue simmering for about 15 minutes, stirring often, until the rice is tender and creamy. Stir through the chopped almonds; remove the vanilla bean, cinnamon stick and lemon zest and discard.

Meanwhile, to make the cherry sauce, put the cherries and their juices, sugar and 60 ml (2 fl oz/¼ cup) water in a saucepan over medium–high heat and stir until the sugar has dissolved. Mix the cornflour with 2 teaspoons cold water until smooth, then stir into the cherries. Bring to the boil, then reduce the heat and simmer for 5 minutes, or until thickened. Stir in the cherry liqueur.

Serve the rice pudding in bowls with the cherry sauce over the top and sprinkle with the crushed vienna almonds. Serve immediately.

Note: It is a Danish tradition to place a whole almond into one bowl of pudding – whoever finds it wins a small Christmas present – such as a marzipan pig!

RICE PUDDING

1 vanilla bean, split and scraped
625 ml (21½ fl oz/2½ cups) full-cream (whole) milk
625 ml (21½ fl oz/2½ cups) pouring (whipping) cream
1 cinnamon stick, halved
⅛ teaspoon ground cardamom
1 strip of lemon zest, white pith removed
220 g (7¾ oz/1 cup) short-grain white rice
110 g (3¾ oz/½ cup) sugar
40 g (1½ oz/¼ cup) blanched almonds, very finely chopped

CHERRY SAUCE

300 g (10½ oz/1½ cups) frozen cherries, defrosted
80 g (2¾ oz/⅓ cup) caster (superfine) sugar
½ teaspoon cornflour (cornstarch)
1½ tablespoons sweet dark cherry liqueur, such as cherry liqueur, or schnapps

vienna almonds or other toffee-coated roasted almonds, lightly crushed, to garnish

POPPY SEED AND WALNUT POTICA WITH COFFEE GLAZE

SERVES 8–10

30 g (1 oz) yeast
60 ml (2 fl oz/¼ cup) warm full-cream (whole) milk, plus 2 teaspoons extra
95 g (3¼ oz/½ cup) soft brown sugar
450 g (1 lb/3 cups) plain (all-purpose) flour
2 egg yolks, beaten
125 g (4½ oz/½ cup) sour cream
40 g (1½ oz) unsalted butter, softened
extra walnut halves, whole or roughly chopped, for decorating
whipped cream, to serve (optional)

Crumble the yeast into a small bowl, add 60 ml (2 fl oz/¼ cup) of the milk, a pinch of salt and ½ teaspoon of the sugar and mash together until smooth. Cover with plastic wrap and set aside in a warm place for about 15 minutes, or until it becomes frothy.

Sift the flour and remaining sugar into a bowl and mix well. Make a well in the centre, pour in the yeast mixture, then add the egg yolk, sour cream and butter and mix thoroughly until you have a soft, slightly sticky dough. Add the extra milk if needed.

Turn the dough out onto a lightly floured work surface and knead for 10–15 minutes, or until smooth and no longer sticky. Place in a bowl, cover with plastic wrap and set aside in a warm place for 1 hour, or until it has doubled in size.

To make the filling, finely grind the poppy seeds in a spice grinder or using a mortar and pestle until the oils are released and aromatic. Put in a saucepan with the milk, butter, vanilla, cinnamon and lemon zest. Cook over medium heat for 5 minutes, stirring constantly, until the poppy seeds have softened. Remove from the heat, then stir in the honey, sugar, rum, walnuts and egg white. Return to the heat and cook on low for a further 8 minutes, or until the mixture is thick. Remove from the heat and allow to cool.

Butter a kugelhopf or bundt tin. Punch down the dough, then roll out into a circle with a 50 cm (20 inch) diameter. Spread the poppy-seed filling over the circle, leaving a 2 cm (¾ inch) border at the outside edge. Roll up the dough as tightly as you can into a log, then place around the prepared cake tin, ensuring the seam side is facing the centre of the tin. Cover and set aside in a warm place for 1 hour, or until puffed up.

While the cake is resting, preheat the oven to 170°C (325°F/Gas 3). Put the cake in the oven and cook for 45 minutes, or until golden brown and hollow when tapped. Cool slightly and turn out onto a wire rack to cool.

When the cake has almost finished cooling make the coffee glaze by combining all the ingredients in a bowl and mixing until smooth and runny, adding a few drops of water if needed. Pour the icing over the top of the cooled cake and allow it to naturally trickle down the sides. Sprinkle the walnuts over the top and allow the icing to set. Serve slices with a dollop of whipped cream, if desired.

Note: Buy poppy seeds from a good spice shop or health food store, not from the supermarket, as they need to be really fresh for optimum flavour and texture.

POPPY SEED AND WALNUT FILLING

100 g (3½ oz/⅔ cup) poppy seeds (see note)

60 ml (2 fl oz/¼ cup) full-cream (whole) milk

50 g (1¾ oz) unsalted butter

1 teaspoon natural vanilla extract

1 teaspoon ground cinnamon

¼ teaspoon finely grated lemon zest

1 tablespoon honey

55 g (2 oz/¼ cup) caster (superfine) sugar

1 tablespoon golden rum

60 g (2¼ oz/½ cup) toasted walnuts, very finely chopped

1 egg white, whisked until thick and foamy

COFFEE GLAZE

185 g (6½ oz/1½ cups) icing (confectioners') sugar, sifted

3 tablespoons freshly brewed coffee, chilled

¾ teaspoon natural vanilla extract

RHUBARB KISEL WITH GINGERBREAD ICE CREAM AND SPECULAAS COOKIES

SERVES 6–8

SPECULAAS COOKIES

300 g (10½ oz/2 cups) plain (all-purpose) flour
¾ teaspoon baking powder
1 tablespoon ground cinnamon
1 teaspoon ground ginger
¼ teaspoon ground cloves
a large pinch of white pepper
1 teaspoon freshly grated nutmeg
½ teaspoon fine sea salt
345 g (12 oz/1½ cups) dark brown sugar
150 g (5½ oz) unsalted butter, cubed
1 large egg, lightly beaten
½ teaspoon natural vanilla extract
45 g (1½ oz/½ cup) flaked almonds (optional)

Start the cookies the day before you wish to serve them. Sift together the flour, baking powder, spices, sea salt and sugar into a bowl. Add the butter and rub into the flour mixture with your fingertips until it resembles breadcrumbs. Add the egg and vanilla and cut into the mixture with a flat-bladed knife until it forms clumps — you can add 1–2 teaspoons water if it is a little dry. Gather together into a ball, cover in plastic wrap, and refrigerate overnight to allow the flavours to develop.

To make the ice cream, put the milk, cream, vanilla, ginger, cinnamon, allspice and cloves in a saucepan over medium–high heat and bring just to the boil. Reduce the heat and simmer for 3 minutes, then remove from the heat, cover and set aside for 15 minutes to allow the flavours to infuse. Strain through a fine sieve into a bowl. Whisk together the egg yolks, molasses and brown sugar, then gradually whisk in the milk mixture. Pour into a clean saucepan and cook over a low–medium heat for about 10 minutes, stirring constantly, until the mixture thickens and easily coats the back of a spoon — do not allow to boil. Cool slightly, then cover and refrigerate until cold. Churn in an ice-cream machine according to the manufacturer's instructions. Alternatively, you can transfer the mixture to a shallow metal tray and freeze, whisking every couple of hours until frozen and creamy. Freeze until ready to serve.

When ready to cook the speculaas, preheat the oven to 170°C (325°F/Gas 3) and line baking trays with baking paper. Take the dough out of the refrigerator, divide in half and roll each half between two sheets of baking paper until about 5 mm (¼ inch) thick. Use a knife to cut into rectangles or use a pastry cutter to stamp out shapes. If using the almonds, sprinkle over the top of each cookie and gently press down to adhere. Place the cookies on the prepared baking trays well spaced to allow for spreading and cook for 15 minutes, or until golden — they will still be a little soft to the touch in the centre but will crisp on cooling. Carefully transfer to wire racks to cool.

While the cookies are baking, make the rhubarb kisel. Finely slice the rhubarb and put in a saucepan with 750 ml (26 fl oz/3 cups) water. Bring to the boil over high heat, then reduce the heat and simmer for 10 minutes, or until the rhubarb is very soft and falls apart. Remove from the heat and cool slightly before transferring to a food processor and blending until smooth. Strain back into a clean saucepan and add the sugar. Stir over medium–high heat until the sugar has dissolved. Dissolve the potato starch in 1 tablespoon of cold water and stir into the rhubarb. Continue stirring for 5 minutes until the mixture boils and thickens slightly, then remove from the heat and allow to cool slightly.

Divide the warm rhubarb kisel between wide shallow serving bowls. Place a scoop of ice cream in the centre and serve with speculaas on the side.

Note: This recipes makes 50 cookies — more than you need — but they are delicious and great on their own with a hot chocolate or coffee and can be stored in an airtight container for a few weeks. They are also used in the spiced cookie cream (page 224).

GINGERBREAD ICE CREAM

375 ml (13 fl oz/1½ cups) full-cream (whole) milk
500 ml (17 fl oz/2 cups) pouring (whipping) cream
1 teaspoon natural vanilla extract
3 teaspoons ground ginger
1 teaspoon ground cinnamon
1 teaspoon ground allspice
a small pinch of ground cloves
8 egg yolks
1½ tablespoons molasses
95 g (3¼ oz/½ cup) soft brown sugar

RHUBARB KISEL

700 g (1 lb 9 oz) fresh rhubarb (about 1 bunch), trimmed
230 g (8½ oz/1 cup) caster (superfine) sugar
3 teaspoons potato starch

APPLE OLIEBOLLEN WITH BUTTERMILK NUTMEG ICE CREAM

SERVES 8

To make the ice cream, heat the cream, buttermilk and vanilla bean and seeds in a saucepan over medium–high heat until it just comes to the boil. Remove from the heat and set aside for 15 minutes to allow the flavours to infuse. Strain through a fine sieve. Beat the egg yolks and sugar until creamy, then gradually whisk in the buttermilk mixture. Place back into a clean saucepan over a low–medium heat and cook for 10 minutes, stirring until the mixture thickens and easily coats the back of a spoon — do not allow to boil. Remove from the heat and cool slightly, then cover and refrigerate until cold. Transfer to an ice-cream machine and freeze according to the manufacturer's instructions. Halfway through freezing, stir in the grated nutmeg. Alternatively, you can transfer the mixture to a shallow metal tray and freeze, whisking every couple of hours until frozen and creamy. Freeze until ready to serve.

To make the apple oliebollen, break up the fresh yeast then mash together with 1 teaspoon of the sugar and 60 ml (2 fl oz/¼ cup) of the warm milk until smooth. Set aside in a warm place for 15 minutes or until frothy. Sift the flour, sea salt and remaining sugar into a bowl and make a well in the centre. Pour in the warm milk, rum, yeast mixture and the egg and mix to combine well. Stir in the raisins, apple and lemon zest combining well. Cover and rest in a warm place until doubled in size — this will take about an hour or so. Bang the bowl a couple of times on the work surface to knock out some of the air.

Fill a deep-fryer or large heavy-based saucepan one-third full with oil and heat to 180°C (350°F), or until a cube of bread dropped into the oil browns in 15 seconds. Using two spoons, carefully drop rounded tablespoons of the mixture into the oil, using one spoon to push the mixture off the other, and cook for about 6 minutes, or until puffed and golden and cooked all the way through. Drain on paper towels and sift icing sugar over the top. Serve with scoops of the ice cream.

Note: Olliebollen are a sweet Dutch fritter popular in the colder months, especially at Christmas.

BUTTERMILK NUTMEG ICE CREAM
375 ml (13 fl oz/1½ cups) pouring (whipping) cream
375 ml (13 fl oz/1½ cups) buttermilk
1 vanilla bean, split and scraped
8 egg yolks
55 g (2 oz/¾ cup) sugar
2 teaspoons freshly grated nutmeg

APPLE OLIEBOLLEN
10 g (¼ oz) fresh yeast
2 tablespoons caster (superfine) sugar
125 ml (4 fl oz/½ cup) lukewarm full-cream (whole) milk
190 g (6¾ oz/1¼ cups) plain (all-purpose) flour
a large pinch sea salt
1 tablespoon rum
1 small egg
1½ tablespoons raisins, chopped
1 granny smith apple, peeled, cored and finely chopped
½ teaspoon finely grated lemon zest
sunflower oil, for deep-frying
icing (confectioners') sugar, for dusting

BUCHE DE NOEL WITH CHESTNUT CREAM

SERVES 10

4 large eggs, at room temperature

145 g (5¼ oz/⅔ cup) caster (superfine) sugar, plus 2 teaspoons extra

½ teaspoon natural vanilla extract

2 tablespoons unsweetened cocoa powder

40 g (1½ oz/⅓ cup) cornflour (cornstarch)

75 g (2½ oz/½ cup) plain (all-purpose) flour

25 g (1 oz/¼ cup) finely ground almonds

a large pinch of baking powder

3 tablespoons almond-flavoured liqueur, such as Amaretto or Crème de Amandes, for brushing

icing (confectioners') sugar, for dusting

fresh holly leaves, for decorating (optional)

CHESTNUT FILLING

210 g (7½ oz/¾ cup) unsweetened chestnut purée

2½ tablespoons almond-flavoured liqueur, such as Amaretto or Crème de Amandes

60 g (2¼ oz/½ cup) icing (confectioners') sugar, sifted

2 tablespoons soft brown sugar

1 teaspoon natural vanilla extract

125 ml (4 fl oz/½ cup) pouring (whipping) cream

Preheat the oven to 200°C (400°F/Gas 6). Line a 25 x 30 cm (10 x 12 inch) Swiss roll (jelly roll) tin with baking paper.

Beat the eggs with electric beaters on high for about 2 minutes or until starting to become thick and creamy. While the motor is still running, add 1 tablespoon of sugar at a time, beating well after each addition. Continue beating for about 10 minutes, or until the sugar has completely dissolved — the mixture should not feel at all gritty when you rub a little between your thumb and finger. Beat in the vanilla.

Sift the cocoa, cornflour, flour, ground almonds and baking powder together twice. Sift half the flour mixture over the egg mixture and carefully fold through with a rubber spatula. Sift the remaining flour mixture over and fold through again, mixing well, but being careful not to beat out all the air. Carefully pour the mixture into the prepared tin and smooth over. Cook in the oven for about 10 minutes, or until golden all over and the top just springs back to the touch. Remove from the oven and invert the cake onto a clean tea towel (dish towel) that has been lined with baking paper and sprinkled with the extra caster sugar. Peel off the baking paper used to line the tin and discard. Brush the top of the cake with a little of the almond liqueur. Using the tea towel to help you, carefully roll up the cake and the baking paper from one long side. Place the roll on a cake rack and allow to cool completely

Meanwhile, to make the filling, use electric beaters to beat together the chestnut purée, almond liqueur, sugars and vanilla until very smooth. Whip the cream to firm peaks, then fold into the chestnut mixture. Cover and chill until ready to use.

When the cake is completely cool, carefully unroll, discarding the baking paper and spread the chestnut cream over the top. Roll up again, place seam side down on a serving platter, and refrigerate until needed.

To make the ganache heat the cream and butter in a saucepan over medium heat until it just comes to the boil. Remove from the heat and stir in both the grated chocolates until they are completely melted and the mixture is smooth and a consistent colour. Tip into a bowl, cool slightly, then cover and refrigerate for about 50 minutes, or until a spreadable consistency.

When ready to ice the cake, use a bread knife to cut, on the diagonal, about a quarter of the cake from one end of the log. Spread a little of the ganache on the cut side of the small piece of cake and adhere it to one side of the log, to make a a small 'branch'. Spread the rest of the ganache over the entire cake, then run a fork over the top to create a bark-like effect, complete with knots. Refrigerate until set, then cover with plastic wrap and refrigerate overnight. If you are tempted to serve straight away — please don't! The cake needs time to rest so it has the right consistency and flavour.

When ready to serve, liberally dust the cake with icing sugar, to represent snow, and garnish as desired, with fresh holly leaves, seasonal flowers or edible berries. Slice with a hot knife dipped in boiling water and then dried.

Variation: For the garnish, it is also popular to dress the yule log with mushroom shapes — either made from marzipan or meringue and dusted with a little cocoa.

CHOCOLATE GANACHE
185 ml (6 fl oz/¾ cup) pouring (whipping) cream
50 g (1¾ oz) unsalted butter
150 g (5½ oz) dark couverture chocolate, grated
150 g (5½ oz) milk couverture chocolate, grated

MARZIPAN BUTTER STOLLEN

SERVES 10–12

85 g (3 oz/⅔ cup) raisins

35 g (1¼ oz/¼ cup) currants

60 g (2¼ oz/¼ cup) glacé cherries, chopped

40 g (1½ oz/¼ cup) finely chopped candied
  lemon peel

80 ml (2½ fl oz/⅓ cup) dark rum

1½ teaspoons ground cinnamon

1½ teaspoons freshly grated nutmeg

30 g (1 oz) fresh yeast

115 g (4 oz/½ cup) caster (superfine) sugar

185 ml (6 fl oz/¾ cup) warm full-cream
  (whole) milk

450 g (1 lb/3 cups) plain (all-purpose) flour

1 egg, at room temperature, lightly beaten

2 teaspoons natural vanilla extract

120 g (4¼ oz) softened unsalted butter, melted,
  plus 40 g (1½ oz), extra

200 g (7 oz) soft marzipan (almond paste)

1 egg yolk

90 g (3¼ oz/¾ cup) icing (confectioners') sugar

Combine the fruit, lemon peel and rum in a bowl. Toss to combine, then cover and set aside overnight, stirring occasionally. Drain off any excess rum before using. Add the cinnamon and nutmeg and stir well.

Crumble the yeast into a small bowl, add ½ teaspoon of the caster sugar and 125 ml (4 fl oz/½ cup) of the warm milk. Mash together until smooth, then leave in a warm place for about 15 minutes, or until frothy. Sift the flour into a large bowl, then stir in the remaining sugar. Make a well in the centre and pour in the yeast mixture. Add the egg, vanilla, remaining milk and melted butter, and mix until you have a soft, sticky dough. Turn out onto a lightly floured work surface and knead for about 5 minutes, or until the mixture comes together and is less sticky. Place in a bowl, cover, and set aside for 1 hour, or until doubled in size.

Punch down the dough, turn out again onto the work surface and quickly knead in the fruit, in three batches, until it is well incorporated. Return to the bowl, cover, and set aside for another 2 hours, or until risen.

Meanwhile, combine the marzipan with the egg yolk and 30 g (1 oz/ ¼ cup) of the icing sugar and mash to combine well. Shape into a log about 3 cm (1¼ inch) wide and refrigerate.

Preheat the oven to 180°C (350°F/Gas 4). Shape the dough into a long oval and roll to make a 20 x 35 cm (8 x 14 inch) rectangle, about 1 cm (½ inch) thick. Make a deep dent along the dough's length, just off-centre, with a rolling pin. Place the marzipan log in the dent. Pull the wider side of the dough over to cover and push into the dough on the opposite side to help adhere. Roll the edge so the join is underneath. Place on a greased and floured baking tray and rest for about 10 minutes. Brush with a little of the extra melted butter and bake for 20 minutes, then reduce the temperature to 160°C (315°F/Gas 2–3) and cook for a further 25 minutes, or until it is golden all over and sounds slightly hollow when tapped.

Remove from the oven, brush over the remaining melted butter until dissolved. Evenly and thickly sift over the remaining icing sugar. Allow to cool, then store in an airtight container or cover with plastic wrap overnight before cutting — this resting is important to achieve the correct texture. The stollen will keep well for about 1 week.

SACHER TORTE WITH APRICOT AND ORANGE CREAM

SERVES 8–10

Preheat the oven to 180°C (350°F/Gas 4). Lightly grease, line and flour a 22 cm (8½ inch) non-stick, spring-form cake tin. Beat the butter, icing sugar and vanilla together in the bowl of an electric mixer, until pale and creamy. With the motor still running, beat in the egg yolks, one at a time. Mix in the melted chocolate and cocoa. Whisk the egg whites with a large pinch of caster sugar until soft peaks form, then continue whisking while gradually adding the remaining caster sugar, until stiff peaks form. Add a spoonful to the chocolate mixture and mix well, then carefully fold in the remaining egg white. Sift the flour over the top and gently fold in, until well combined, but be careful not to beat out the air.

Carefully pour into the prepared tin and smooth over. Bake for about 30–35 minutes, or until a skewer inserted into the centre of the cake comes out clean. Cool completely in the tin on a wire rack, then remove from the tin. Carefully trim so that the top is flat. Using an electric knife or sharp bread knife, carefully cut horizontally through the centre of the cake to form two even layers.

Heat the jam and brandy over medium heat until the jam melts and the mixture is glazy. Brush half of the jam glaze over the cut side of the bottom cake layer, then place the top layer back to its original position so the cake is as level as possible. Brush the remaining jam glaze over the top and sides of the cake. Dry on a wire rack over a tray.

To make the glaze, put the sugar and 125 ml (4 fl oz/½ cup) water in a heavy-based saucepan over medium heat and stir until the sugar dissolves. Bring to the boil and cook for about 5 minutes, without stirring, or until syrupy. Remove from the heat and cool for 2 minutes, then add the chocolate and stir with a metal spoon for 6–8 minutes, or until thick enough to hold a letter 's' when drizzled back onto the mixture. Working quickly, pour the glaze onto the centre of the cake and allow it to naturally flow over the sides. Smooth around the sides with a palette knife dipped in hot water then dried quickly so it is hot but not wet.

While the glaze sets, whip the cream and fold through the glacé apricots, brandy and orange zest. Cover and refrigerate until ready to serve. Use a knife dipped in hot water to cut the cake into wedges and serve with the apricot and orange cream.

125 g (4½ oz) unsalted butter
125 g (4½ oz/1 cup) icing (confectioners') sugar
1 teaspoon natural vanilla extract
5 eggs, separated, at room temperature
150 g (5½ oz) dark couverture chocolate, melted and cooled slightly
1 tablespoon unsweetened cocoa powder, sifted
55 g (2 oz/¼ cup) caster (superfine) sugar
150 g (5½ oz/1 cup) plain (all-purpose) flour
160 g (5½ oz/½ cup) good-quality apricot jam
2 tablespoons apricot brandy

GLAZE
230 g (8½ oz/1 cup) caster (superfine) sugar
175 g (6 oz) dark couverture chocolate, grated

APRICOT AND ORANGE CREAM
375ml (13 fl oz/1½ cups) pouring (whipping) cream
100 g (3½ oz) glacé apricots, finely diced
3 teaspoon apricot brandy
1 teaspoon finely grated orange zest

BAKED CHEESECAKE WITH FROZEN CRANBERRIES AND CARAMEL

SERVES 8–10

CHEESECAKE BASE

150 g (5¼ oz) unsalted butter, diced

80 g (2¾ oz/⅓ cup) caster (superfine) sugar

1 tablespoon sour cream

5 egg yolks

150 g (5½ oz/1 cup) plain (all-purpose) flour, sifted

CHEESECAKE FILLING

375 g (13 oz/1½ cups) quark (qvark) or cream cheese (see note, page 163)

375 g (13 oz/1½ cups) sour cream

250 g (9 oz/1 cup) ricotta cheese, drained

170 g (6 oz/¾ cup) caster (superfine) sugar

2 whole eggs

2 tablespoons potato flour

¼ teaspoon baking powder

1 teaspoon freshly grated nutmeg

1½ teaspoons finely grated orange or lemon zest

2 teaspoons natural vanilla extract

250 g (9 oz/2 cups) frozen cranberries, red currants or blackberries, do not thaw

CARAMEL SAUCE

250 ml (9 fl oz/1 cup) pouring (whipping) cream

95 g (3¼ oz/½ cup) soft brown sugar

1 teaspoon molasses

To make the cheesecake base, beat the butter, sugar and a pinch of salt in a bowl using electric beaters on high speed for 6 minutes, or until pale and creamy. Add the sour cream and 1 egg yolk and beat until smooth. Fold in the flour, mixing well to form a soft dough. Line the base of a 23 cm (9 inch) spring-form cake tin with baking paper, then tip the dough into the base of the tin and press down evenly. Prick the base all over with a fork. Chill for 30 minutes, or until firm.

Preheat the oven to 170°C (325°F/Gas 3). Cook the cheesecake base for 25 minutes, or until just dry to the touch. Remove from the heat and cool in the tin on a wire rack. Reduce the oven temperature to 150°C (300°F/Gas 2).

To make the cheesecake filling, put the quark, sour cream, ricotta and sugar into the bowl of an electric mixer and beat on high speed for 10 minutes, or until very smooth. Beat in the remaining 4 egg yolks until well combined, then add the whole eggs, one at a time, beating until smooth. Sift over the potato flour, baking powder and nutmeg and fold in the zest and vanilla. Mix well and spoon over the base in the tin. Place on a baking tray.

Put a heatproof bowl of water on the bottom of the oven. Bake the cheesecake for 55–60 minutes, or until just set on top — the cheesecake should still wobble just a little in the middle. Remove from the heat, cool to room temperature in the tin on a wire rack. Wrap in plastic wrap and refrigerate for at least 8 hours or overnight.

When ready to serve, run a hot knife around the tin to loosen the cheesecake. Remove the sides of the tin, then carefully remove the base and transfer the cheesecake to a serving plate.

To make the caramel sauce, place all the ingredients in a heavy-based saucepan over medium–high heat and stir until the sugar dissolves. Bring to the boil, then reduce the heat and simmer for 3 minutes, or until thickened slightly — do not allow the caramel to thicken too much or it will set in clumps when it hits the frozen cranberries. Allow to cool slightly.

Pile the frozen cranberries on top of the cheesecake, then drizzle over the hot caramel sauce (which will help to thaw the cranberries — but it is this half-frozen, half-hot combination we are looking for) and serve immediately. Serve with shots of cranberry vodka or liqueur.

CHRISTMAS KRINGLE

SERVES 10–12

20 g (¾ oz) fresh yeast
80 g (2¾ oz/⅓ cup) caster (superfine) sugar
250 ml (9 fl oz/1 cup) warm full-cream
  (whole) milk
125 g (4½ oz) unsalted butter
425 g (15 oz/2¾ cups) plain (all-purpose) flour
1 egg yolk, lightly beaten

CUSTARD FILLING

2½ tablespoons raisins, chopped
1½ tablespoons brandy
310 ml (10¾ fl oz/1¼ cups) full-cream
  (whole) milk
2½ tablespoons plain (all-purpose) flour
2 tablespoons caster (superfine) sugar
¼ teaspoon finely grated lemon zest
½ teaspoon natural vanilla extract
¼ teaspoon natural almond extract
4 egg yolks, lightly beaten

Crumble the yeast into a bowl with 2 teaspoons of the sugar and pour over 60 ml (2 fl oz/¼ cup) of the warm milk. Mash together until smooth, cover with plastic wrap, and set aside in a warm place for 15 minutes or until frothy. Meanwhile, gently melt the butter in a saucepan with the remaining milk over low heat. Remove from the heat and set aside.

Sift the flour into a large bowl with a large pinch of salt. Stir in the remaining sugar and make a well in the centre. Pour the yeast mixture into the well with the egg yolk and the melted butter mixture and mix well until a soft dough forms. Cover with plastic wrap and set aside in a warm place for about 1 hour, or until doubled in size.

While the dough rests, make the custard filling. Combine the raisins and brandy and set aside for 30 minutes before draining and squeezing out any excess moisture. Meanwhile, heat the milk in a small saucepan over medium heat until it just starts to simmer. Sift the flour and sugar into a bowl, then gradually whisk in the warm milk until smooth. Return the mixture to the saucepan, add the lemon zest and vanilla and almond extracts, and place over high heat, stirring for 2 minutes, until quite thick. Remove from the heat, cool slightly, then whisk in the egg yolks. Place back over a low heat and stir for 2 minutes, or until thickened again. Stir in the drained raisins. Remove from the heat, cool slightly, then cover with baking paper and refrigerate until well chilled.

Preheat the oven to 180°C (350°F/Gas 4). When the dough has doubled in size, punch it down and roll out to make a 16 x 90 cm (6¼ x 35½ inch) rectangle, about 5 mm (¼ inch) thick. The long sides should be in front of you, the short sides left and right. Trim to neaten if necessary. Evenly dollop the cooled custard along the length of the dough, just off centre on the side furthest away from you. Leaving a 2 cm (¾ inch) border at each short end, spread the custard dollops along the line so that it is about 5 mm (¼ inch) thick, then take the edge of the dough closest to you and fold it up and over the custard, pressing to seal. Take the two short edges and gently slide them along the bench towards you, forming an arc, then lift them up and cross them over and away from you forming a large pretzel-like shape. Tuck the short ends under the arc and press down all over the dough to flatten slightly. Carefully slide onto an extra-large baking tray lined with baking paper.

To make the almond topping, combine the flour, sugar, almonds and spices and thoroughly mix in the melted butter — you should have a crumbly mixture. Sprinkle liberally over the kringle, pressing down to help adhere.

Cook in the oven for 40 minutes, or until golden all over. Allow to cool slightly and serve cut into slices with whipped cream or ice cream; it is also great served on its own with coffee.

Note: If you don't have a baking tray large enough to cook the dough, you can make two kringles on two separate trays. You will need to reduce the rectangle measurements by half and bake the kringles for a little less time.

ALMOND TOPPING
50 g (1¾ oz/⅓ cup) plain (all-purpose) flour
115 g (4 oz/½ cup) caster (superfine) sugar
45 g (1½ oz/½ cup) flaked almonds
¼ teaspoon ground cardamom
½ teaspoon ground cinnamon
90 g (3¼ oz) unsalted butter, melted

LEBKUCHEN BREAD OF LIFE

MAKES 18

Heat the honey, molasses and brown sugar in a saucepan over medium heat, stirring for 5 minutes, or until the sugar has dissolved.

Sift the flour, bicarbonate of soda, a pinch of salt and the spices together into a large bowl. Make a well in the centre and pour in the honey mixture. Stir to combine, then add the candied peel and egg and mix well to combine — you should have a soft, sticky dough. Cover with plastic wrap and refrigerate overnight.

Preheat the oven to 170°C (325°F/Gas 3). Bring the dough back to room temperature, then roll out between two pieces of baking paper until 8 mm (3/8 inch) thick. Stamp out shapes using a large heart-shaped cutter (it helps to dip the cutter and your fingers in water so the dough doesn't stick). If you can't find a cutter, trace a heart or any other shape you like onto a piece of baking paper, then cut it out, lay it over the rolled dough and using a sharp knife cut around the edges — you should make about 18 hearts in total.

Space the hearts out on baking trays lined with baking paper. Place the almonds decoratively around the edges of half of the hearts. Cook for about 12–13 minutes, or until the biscuits slowly spring back when pressed with your finger.

Transfer to wire racks to cool, then decorate the unadorned hearts with melted chocolate, piping festive patterns or words, or drizzling swirls over the tops of the hearts. Allow to set. Store the biscuits in an airtight container, in a cool place for up to 1 month. You can serve these straight away as a firm, chewy treat, however many people prefer to leave them for a week or two to allow the lebkuchen to soften and the flavours to mellow slightly.

Variation: A simple lemon glaze or icing can be used to top the lebkuchen instead of chocolate (page 65).

Note: If using the biscuits as Christmas decorations, pierce holes in the tops of the lebkuchen with a skewer before placing on the tray and cooking.

175 g (6 oz/½ cup) honey
175 g (6 oz/½ cup) molasses
95 g (3¼ oz/½ cup) soft brown sugar
375 g (13 oz/2½ cups) plain (all-purpose) flour
½ teaspoon bicarbonate of soda (baking soda)
1 teaspoon ground ginger
1½ teaspoons ground cinnamon
¾ teaspoon ground cloves
1½ teaspoons freshly grated nutmeg
1 teaspoon ground allspice
¼ teaspoon ground aniseed
1 tablespoon finely chopped candied lemon peel
1 tablespoon finely chopped candied orange peel
1 egg, beaten
blanched almonds, for decorating
melted dark and/or white chocolate, for piping (optional)

ACKNOWLEDGMENTS

As always, a heartfelt thank you to the supremely talented and extraordinary Ms Kay Scarlett. Thank you also to Matt and Clare Handbury, Juliet Rogers and the MB Acquisitions committee. I so appreciate, once again, not only the financial investment but the faith in the concept.

To the remaining Murdoch Books family — thank you, not only for producing such beautiful books, but for recently welcoming me back into the fold with opened arms

To the passionate and talented Alice Adams, Ross Dobson, Vicky Harris and Chris Tate — thank you all so very much for enduring the demands for painstaking accuracy during the recipe testing process and also to Janine Flew for your valuable feedback at tastings.

To the gorgeous and dedicated Peta Dent, super-efficient Chrissy Freer and uber-baker Kathy Knudsen — thank you all so very much for making my recipes look so damn delicious!

Brett Stevens and Lynsey Fryers — you have completely blown me away — the lengths you both went to in order to capture the vision of this title were simply phenomenal. I still have a little fake snow in my hair. Thanks guys!

Jacqueline Blanchard — you may have abandoned Sydney for higher ground but I hope you never give up editing our cook books — thank you so much for your words of encouragement and supreme levels of accuracy and professionalism.

Crossman! I have said it before and I will say it again — you are a unique and talented being. I can't thank you enough for the effort and design passion you have injected into this project (and for all your books, for that matter!), for your patience in having to deal with an 'in-house' author with very definite ideas, and finally but not least for your friendship and warped sense of humour. Just promise to keep that butter knife away from me!

And finally to my dear family and friends — thank you all for your patience and understanding. As you all know, work has been crazy busy, but things are slowly getting back on track — I promise! To the many friends far and wide who aided my S&S reseach — a very hearty thank you, particularly to Julie and Moo for their extended hospitality and to Noel for the most spectacular alpine soujourn (including the bare-footed bbq in the snow!) — you can take the girl out of Australia but ...

This book is dedicated to all the 'little people' in my life who teach me so much about myself — especially Jake, Chloe, Jaslyn and Tia xxxx.

INDEX

A

almond hot chocolate 81
almond-crusted schnitzel with pickled
    cabbage 109
apples
    apple horseradish 131
    apple and lingonberry crisps 152
    apple olliebollen with buttermilk nutmeg ice
        cream 265
    bircher muesli pancakes with cranberry apple
        compote and yoghurt 94
    potato and apple croquettes 186
    roast goose with apple, cider vinegar gravy and
        golden potatoes 236–7
    warm apple toddy 76
apricot dumplings, golden, with orange poppy
    seed ice cream 218
Akvavit (Aquavit) 29

B

bacon
    bacon rösti with poached eggs and thyme
        hollandaise 96–7
    slow-baked brown beans with spice-roasted
        bacon 118
beans
    balsamic-glazed veal sweetbreads with white
        bean and sage fritters 176–7
    beef with foie gras, spiced cocoa sauce and
        vanilla-scented beans 188
    borlotti and chestnut soup with scallops and
        parsley oil 171
    slow-baked brown beans with spice-roasted
        bacon 118
beef
    beef fillet in parmesan pastry with truffle
        butter sauce 206–7
    beef with foie gras, spiced cocoa sauce and
        vanilla-scented beans 188
    beer, orange and spice braised short ribs with
        walnut dumplings 106
    meatballs with vodka dill cream sauce 141
    pot au feu 205
    sauerbraten with bread dumplings 112–13
beer, orange and spice braised short ribs with
    walnut dumplings 106
beer-cooked bratwurst hot dogs with sweet and
    spicy mustard 42
beetroot
    beetroot relish 210

(beetroot continued)
    beetroot salad 38
    borscht with horseradish cream 20
    poached veal with beetroot spaetzle and
        herbed cream 190–1
berries
    apple and lingonberry crisps 152
    bircher muesli pancakes with cranberry apple
        compote and yoghurt 94
    cheesecake, baked, with frozen cranberries
        and caramel 272
bigos hunter's stew 251
bircher muesli pancakes with cranberry apple
    compote and yoghurt 94
biscuits
    lebkuchen bread of life 277
    speculaas cookies 262–3
bitterballen 12
blinis, buckwheat blini platter 174
borlotti and chestnut soup with scallops and
    parsley oil 171
borscht with horseradish cream 20
bread
    marzipan butter stollen 270
    poppy seed and walnut potica with coffee glaze
        258–9
buche de Noel with chestnut cream 266–7
buckwheat
    buckwheat blini platter 174
    savoury buckwheat kasha with dilled
        mushrooms 100
buttered balsam 79
buttermilk nutmeg ice cream 265
butters
    chestnut, honey and fennel 59
    egg and anchovy butter 26
    mustard butter 23
    orange whipped butter 93
    prawn, caviar and red onion butter 240

C

cabbage
    almond-crusted schnitzel with pickled
        cabbage 109
    bigos hunter's stew 251
    cabbage rolls 142–3
    cotechino with pumpkin sformato, cavolo nero
        and mustard fruit dressing 182–3
    crisp roast pork with spiced red cabbage and
        apple horseradish 131

(cabbage continued)
    one pot lamb and cabbage 105
    pork and cabbage cakes with sweet onion
        relish 101
    potato and cabbage cakes 249
    roasted rosemary squab with red wine and
        cabbage risotto 195
    salmon with red wine sauce on sautéed
        cabbage and speck 213
cakes
    buche de Noel with chestnut cream 266–7
    cheesecake, baked, with frozen cranberries
        and caramel 272
    honeycake snowballs with fig and buttered rum
        sauce 216–17
    marzipan butter stollen 270
    poppy seed and walnut potica with coffee glaze
        258–9
    raisin ale cake with walnut streusel topping 69
    Sacher torte with apricot and orange cream 271
    saffron and coriander scrolls with lemon
        glaze 65
caper and lemon rösti-crusted perch with
    creamed spinach and leek 197
caraway roast pork rack, pear sauce and mustard
    onion mash 244–5
carrot and molasses bake 230
cauliflower, grilled oysters with cauliflower
    custard and caviar 168
cheese
    cheese fondue 16
    cottage cheese and plum dumplings with
        cinnamon walnuts 155
    quark fritters with honey syrup 163
    three-cheese polenta pizza with sweet onions
        and walnuts 56
cheesecake, baked, with frozen cranberries and
    caramel 272
cherry mint warmer 75
cherry relish 229
cherry strudel 158–9
chestnut, honey and fennel butter 59
chestnut stuffing 232
chicken
    chicken fricassée 117
    coriander roast chicken with walnut sauce 151
    dilled chicken and vegetable broth with
        noodles 33
    kurnik chicken pie 134–5
    paprika chicken 110

(chicken continued)
truffled chicken breasts with leeks and a
    Champagne cream sauce 252-3
chocolate
    almond hot chocolate 81
    chocolate fondue 156
    chocolate ganache 267
    doughnut balls with mocha 'soup' 60-1
    panettone, chocolate and marshmallow
        melts 66
    warm chocolate and walnut pancake torte 164
Christmas kringle 274-5
cloudberry sauce 187
coriander roast chicken with walnut sauce 151
cotechino with pumpkin sformato, cavolo nero
    and mustard fruit dressing 182-3
cottage cheese and plum dumplings with
    cinnamon walnuts 155
cranberry apple compote 94
crumble, winter vegetable 49
cucumbers, pickled 26
curry remoulade 55
custard
    Christmas kringle 274-5
    grilled oysters with cauliflower custard and
        caviar 168
    liquorice custards with coconut-lime
        macaroons and plums 221

D
Danish rice pudding with cherry sauce 257
desserts
    apple and lingonberry crisps 152
    apple oliebollen with buttermilk nutmeg ice
        cream 265
    bircher muesli pancakes with cranberry apple
        compote and yoghurt 94
    buche de noel with chestnut ice cream 266-67
    cheesecake, baked, with frozen cranberries
        and caramel 272
    cherry strudel 158-9
    cottage cheese dumplings with cinnamon
        walnuts 155
    chocolate fondue 156
    creamed polenta with cinnamon prunes 90
    Danish rice pudding with cherry sauce 257
    doughnut balls with mocha 'soup' 60-1
    golden apricot dumplings with orange poppy
        seed ice cream 218
    honeycake snowballs with fig and buttered
        rum sauce 216-17
    liquorice custards with coconut-lime
        macaroons and plums 221
    molten Black Forest puddings with cherry
        compote and Kirsch cream 223
    panettone, chocolate and marshmallow melts
        66

(desserts continued)
    prune-filled crepes baked in caramel with
        spiced cookie cream 224
    pumpkin-seed marzipan pastries with glacé
        pumpkin 222
    quark fritters with honey syrup 163
    raisin ale cake with walnut streusel topping 9
    rhubarb kisel with gingerbread ice cream and
        saffron and coriander scrolls with lemon glaze
        65
    Sacher torte with apricot and orange
        cream 271
    speculaas cookies 262-3
    spiced buttermilk waffles with rhubarb
        molasses and orange whipped butter 93
dill chicken and vegetable broth with
    noodles 33
doughnut balls with mocha 'soup' 60-1
drinks
    almond hot chocolate 81
    buttered balsam 79
    cherry mint warmer 75
    elderflower, gin and lemon sipper 84
    gingerbread-spice coffee 80
    honey and saffron liqueur 87
    mulled wine 72
    warm apple toddy 76
duck
    bigos hunter's stew 251
    spiced duck breast with walnut-crusted potato
        and apple croquettes and cloudberry
        sauce 186-7
    duck liver and Tokaji mousse with muscatels
        and walnut wafers 172-3
dumplings
    bread dumplings 112-13
    cottage cheese and plum dumplings 155
    golden apricot dumplings 218
    goulash soup with caraway dumplings 15
    walnut dumplings 106

E
eggplant, wholemeal piroshki with lamb and 52-3
eggs
    bacon rösti with poached eggs and thyme
        hollandaise 96-7
    egg and anchovy butter 26
elderflower, gin and lemon sipper 84

F
fennel
    liquorice lamb with roasted fennel and carrots,
        havarti cream and sweet carrot jus 199
    mussels in a fennel-scented broth 29
    polenta loaf with chestnut, honey and fennel
        butter 59
    sticky plum and fennel pork ribs 32

fig sauce 216
fish
    caper and lemon rösti-crusted perch with
        creamed spinach and leek 197
    fish cakes 38, 55
    fish frikadeller with curry remoulade 55
    Swedish open burger with beetroot salad 38
    white fish pudding with prawn sauce 180
    see also seafood
flatbreads, potato, with smoked salmon 26
fondues
    cheese 16
    chocolate 156
fritters
    quark fritters with honey syrup 163
    white bean and sage fritters 176

G
garlic
    garlicky pelmeni with brown butter, herbs and
        yoghurt 128-9
    spiced wheat beer and bread soup with garlic
        cream 57
ginger ice cream 216
gingerbread-spice coffee 80
gingerbread-spice glazed ham with cherry relish 229
gjetost 211
goose, roast, with apple, cider vinegar gravy and
    golden potatoes 236-7
goulash soup with caraway dumplings 15
gremolata 125

H
ham
    gingerbread-spice glazed ham with cherry
        relish 229
    herbed pretzels with honey-glazed ham and
        mustard butter 22-3
    tartiflette 41
herb-stuffed rolled veal breast baked in cream 243
herbed pretzels with honey-glazed ham and
    mustard butter 22-3
honeycake snowballs with fig and buttered rum
    sauce 216-17
honey and saffron liqueur 87
horseradish cream 20
hot dogs, beer-cooked bratwurst, with sweet
    and spicy mustard 42
hotpot, Nordic seafood 121

I
ice cream
    buttermilk nutmeg ice cream 265
    ginger ice cream 216
    gingerbread ice cream 262-3
    orange poppy seed ice cream 218
Italian-style meatloaf with lentils 104

J

Janssen's temptation 148

juniper-dusted venison fillet with gjetost sauce and beetroot relish 210–11

K

Karelian open pies 30

kasha, savoury buckwheat, with dilled mushrooms 100

kurnik chicken pie 134–5

L

lamb

    liquorice lamb with roasted fennel and carrots, havarti cream and sweet carrot jus 199

    one pot lamb and cabbage 105

    slow-cooked lamb shanks with Janssen's temptation 148

    wholemeal piroshki with lamb and eggplant 52–3

lasagne verde 146–7

leeks

    caper and lemon rösti-crusted perch with creamed spinach and leeks 197

    truffled chicken breasts with leeks and a Champagne cream sauce 252–3

lebkuchen bread of life 277

lentils, Italian-style meatloaf with 104

liquorice custards with coconut–lime macaroons and plums 221

liquorice lamb with roasted fennel and carrots, havarti cream and sweet carrot jus 199

M

macaroons, coconut–lime 221

marzipan butter stollen 270

meatballs with vodka dill cream sauce 141

meatloaf, Italian-style, with lentils 104

molten black forest puddings with cherry compote and kirsch cream 223

mulled wine 72

mushrooms

    mushroom and barley soup with pickled mushroom cream 45

    savoury buckwheat kasha with dilled mushrooms 100

mussels in a fennel-scented broth 29

mustard

    mustard butter 23

    mustard fruit dressing 183

    mustard onion mash 244–5

    mustard-roasted turkey with speck potatoes and honey sauce 115

    sweet and spicy mustard 42

N

noodles

    dilled chicken and vegetable broth with noodles 33

    paprika pork cutlets with red pepper sauce and noodle kugel 122

    Nordic seafood hotpot 121

nuts

    rosemary and spice chestnuts, almonds and hazelnuts 19

see also chestnut; walnuts

O

one-pot lamb and cabbage 105

onions

    mustard onion mash 244–5

    rich onion soup 37

    sweet onion relish 101

    three-cheese polenta pizza with sweet onions 56

orange poppy seed ice cream 218

osso bucco with saffron risotto 124–5

oysters, grilled, with cauliflower custard and caviar 168

P

pancakes

    bircher muesli pancakes with cranberry apple compote and yoghurt 94

    prune-filled crepes baked in caramel with spiced cookie cream 224

    warm chocolate and walnut pancake torte 164

paprika chicken 110

paprika pork cutlets with red pepper sauce and noodle kugel 122

parsley oil 171

peas

    creamed peas 240

    spicy split pea soup with smoked ham 36

pelmeni, garlicky, with brown butter, herbs and yoghurt 128–9

pheasant in plum brandy with potato and cabbage pancakes and prune sauce 248–9

pies

    Karelian open pies 30

    kurnik chicken pie 134–5

    pork in milk with polenta crust 116

piroshki, wholemeal, with lamb and eggplant 52–3

pizza, three-cheese polenta pizza with sweet onions and walnuts 56

polenta

    creamed polenta with cinnamon prunes 90

    polenta loaf with chestnut, honey and fennel butter 59

    pork in milk with polenta crust 116

    three-cheese polenta pizza with sweet onions and walnuts 56

poppy seed and walnut potica with coffee glaze 258–9

pork

    almond-crusted schnitzel with pickled cabbage 109

    bitterballen 12

    cabbage rolls 142–3

    caraway roast pork rack, pear sauce and mustard onion mash 244–5

    crisp roast pork with spiced red cabbage and apple horseradish 131

    garlicky pelmeni with brown butter, herbs and yoghurt 128–9

    meatballs with vodka dill cream sauce 141

    paprika pork cutlets with red pepper sauce and noodle kugel 122

    pork and cabbage cakes with sweet onion relish 101

    pork in milk with polenta crust 116

    rolled pistachio-stuffed pork loin with carrot and molasses bake 230

    sticky plum and fennel pork ribs 32

pot au feu 205

potatoes

    cardamom caramel potatoes 240

    Janssen's temptation 148

    mustard onion mash 244–5

    mustard-roasted turkey with speck potatoes and honey sauce 115

    potato and apple croquettes 186

    potato and cabbage pancakes 248–9

    potato flatbreads with smoked salmon 26–7

    tartiflette 41

potica, poppy seed and walnut, with coffee glaze 258–9

prawn, caviar and red onion butter 240

prawn sauce 180

pretzels, herbed, with honey-glazed ham and mustard butter 22–3

prunes

    creamed polenta with cinnamon prunes 90

    pheasant in plum brandy with potato and cabbage pancakes and prune sauce 248–9

    prune-filled crepes baked in caramel with spiced cookie cream 224

pumpkin

    cotechino with pumpkin sformato, cavolo nero and mustard fruit dressing 182–3

    pumpkin-seed marzipan pastries 222

Q

quark fritters with honey syrup 163

R

rabbit in red wine with spinach canederli 138–9
raisin ale cake with walnut streusel topping 69
Reblochon 41
rhubarb
    rhubarb kisel with gingerbread ice cream and
      speculaas cookies 262–3
    spiced buttermilk waffles with rhubarb
      molasses and orange whipped butter 93
rice
    Danish rice pudding with cherry sauce 257
    Karelian open pies 30
    osso bucco with saffron risotto 124–5
    roasted rosemary squab with red wine and
      cabbage risotto 195
rosemary and spice chestnuts, almonds and
    hazelnuts 19

S

Sacher torte with apricot and orange cream 271
saffron and coriander scrolls with lemon glaze 65
salmon
    potato flatbreads with smoked salmon 26–7
    salmon with red wine sauce on sautéed
      cabbage and speck 213
    whole roast salmon with skagen butter,
      cardamom caramel potatoes and creamed
      peas 240–1
sandwiches
    pan-fried sandwiches 46
sauces
    caramel sauce 224
    Champagne cream sauce 252–3
    cherry sauce 257
    cloudberry sauce 186–7
    fig sauce 216
    herbed cream 190
    honey sauce 115
    pear sauce 244
    prawn sauce 180–1
    prune sauce 249
    red wine sauce 213
    spiced cocoa sauce 188
    thyme hollandaise 96
    truffle butter sauce 207
    walnut sauce 151
    wheat beer sauce 202
sauerbraten with bread dumplings 112–3
sausage
    beer-cooked bratwurst hot dogs with sweet
      and spicy mustard 42
    cotechino with pumpkin sformato, cavolo nero
      and mustard fruit dressing 182–3
    pot au feu 205
schnitzel, almond-crusted, with pickled cabbage 109

seafood
    borlotti and chestnut soup with scallops and
      parsley oil 171
    grilled oysters with cauliflower custard and
      caviar 168
    mussels in a fennel-scented broth 29
    Nordic seafood hotpot 121
    white fish pudding with prawn sauce 180
    see also fish
soup
    borlotti and chestnut soup with scallops and
      parsley oil 171
    borscht with horseradish cream 20
    dilled chicken and vege broth with noodles 33
    goulash soup with caraway dumplings 15
    mushroom and barley soup with pickled
      mushroom cream 45
    mussels in a fennel-scented broth 29
    rich onion soup with cheese toasts 37
    spiced wheat beer and bread soup with garlic
      cream 57
    spicy split pea soup with smoked ham 36
speculaas cookies 262–3
spiced buttermilk waffles with rhubarb molasses
    and orange whipped butter 93
spiced cocoa sauce 188
spiced wheat beer and bread soup 57
spicy split pea soup with smoked ham 36
spinach
    caper and lemon rösti-crusted perch with
      creamed spinach and leek 197
    lasagne verde 146–7
    rabbit in red wine with spinach canederli
      138–9
squab, roasted rosemary squab with red wine and
    cabbage risotto 195
sticky plum and fennel pork ribs 32
Swedish open burger with beetroot salad 38
sweet potato
    venison stroganoff with sweet potato straws 196
    winter vegetable crumble 49
sweetbreads, balsamic glazed veal, with white
    bean and sage fritters 176

T

tartiflette 41
truffle butter sauce 207
truffled chicken breasts with leeks and a
    Champagne cream sauce 252–3
turkey
    cabbage rolls 142–3
    mustard-roasted turkey with speck potatoes
      and honey sauce 115
    roast turkey with chestnut stuffing and Vin
      Santo grape sauce 232–3

V

vanilla sugar 61
veal
    balsamic-glazed veal sweetbreads with white
      bean and sage fritters 176–7
    bitterballen 12
    herb-stuffed veal breast baked in cream 243
    lasagne verde 146–7
    osso bucco with saffron risotto 124
    poached veal with beetroot spaetzle and
      herbed cream 190–1
    veal cutlets with wheat beer sauce and winter
      vegetable strudel 202
venison
    juniper-dusted venison fillet with gjetost sauce
      and beetroot relish 210–11
    venison stroganoff with sweet potato straws
      196

W

waffles, spiced buttermilk, with rhubarb molasses
    and orange whipped butter 93
walnuts
    coriander roast chicken with walnut sauce 151
    cottage cheese and plum dumplings with
      cinnamon walnuts 155
    poppy seed and walnut potica with coffee glaze
      258–9
    raisin ale cake with walnut streusel topping 9
    three-cheese polenta pizza with sweet onions
      and walnuts 56
    walnut dumplings 106
    warm chocolate and walnut pancake torte 164
wheat beer sauce 202
wholemeal piroshki with lamb and eggplant 52–3
winter vegetable crumble 49
winter vegetable strudel 202

Published in 2009 by Murdoch Books Pty Limited

Murdoch Books Australia
Pier 8/9, 23 Hickson Road
Millers Point NSW 2000
Phone: +61 (0) 2 8220 2000
Fax: +61 (0) 2 8220 2558
www.murdochbooks.com.au

Murdoch Books UK Limited
Erico House, 6th Floor
93–99 Upper Richmond Road
Putney, London SW15 2TG
Phone: +44 (0) 20 8785 5995
Fax: +44 (0) 20 8785 5985
www.murdochbooks.co.uk

Chief Executive: Juliet Rogers
Publishing Director: Kay Scarlett

Publisher – Food: Jane Lawson
Project manager and editor: Jacqueline Blanchard
Concept and design: Reuben Crossman
Photographer: Brett Stevens
Food Stylist: Lynsey Fryers
Food Preparation: Peta Dent
Production: Kita George

National Library of Australia Cataloguing-in-
Publication Data:

Author: Lawson, Jane.
Title: Snowflakes and Schnapps / Jane Lawson.
ISBN: 9781921259029 (hardback)
Subjects: Cookery. Cookery, European.
Cookery (Wine).
Dewey Number: 641.594

A catalogue record for this book is available from
the British Library.

Colour separation by Colour Chiefs
Printed by 1010 Printing International Limited.
in 2009. PRINTED IN CHINA.

IMPORTANT: Those who might be at risk from
the effects of salmonella poisoning (the elderly,
pregnant women, young children and those
suffering from immune deficiency diseases)
should consult their doctor with any concerns
about eating raw eggs.

OVEN GUIDE: You may find cooking times vary
depending on the oven you are using. For fan-
forced ovens, as a general rule, set the oven
temperature to 20°C (35°F) lower than indicated
in the recipe.